The Creative Writing MFA Handbook

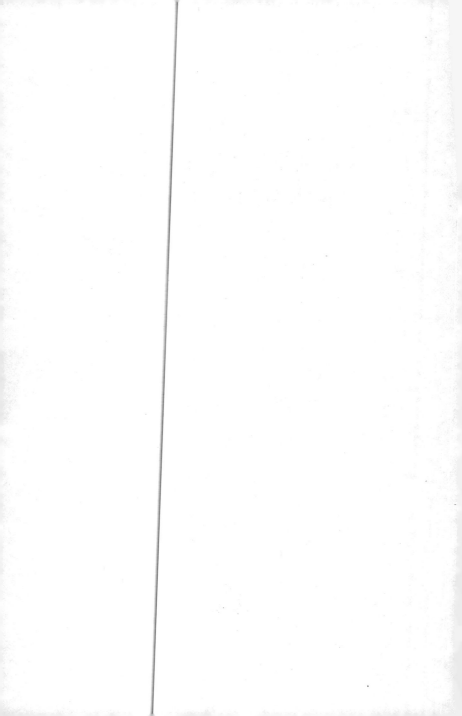

The Creative Writing MFA Handbook

A GUIDE FOR PROSPECTIVE GRADUATE STUDENTS

Second Edition

Tom Kealey

with essays by
Seth Abramson, Erika Dreifus,
Adam Johnson, and Ed Schwarzschild

continuum

NEW YORK • LONDON

The Continuum International Publishing Group Inc
80 Maiden Lane, New York, NY 10038

The Continuum International Publishing Group Ltd
The Tower Building, 11 York Road, London SE1 7NX

www.continuumbooks.com

Library of Congress Cataloging-in-Publication Data

Kealey, Tom.
The creative writing MFA handbook : a guide for prospective
graduate students / Tom Kealey.
    p. cm.
 ISBN 0-8264-1850-3 (hardcover)—ISBN 0-8264-1817-1 (pbk.)
 ISBN 978-0-8264-2886-8 (paperback : alk. paper; 2nd edition)
1. Creative writing (Higher education)—United States—Handbooks,
manuals, etc. 2. Graduate students—United States—Handbooks,
manuals, etc. I. Title.
PE1405.U6K43 2005
808'.042071173—dc22
                2005025228

Printed in the United States of America

05 06 07 08 09 10   10 9 8 7 6 5 4 3 2 1

*For my students
and
my teachers*

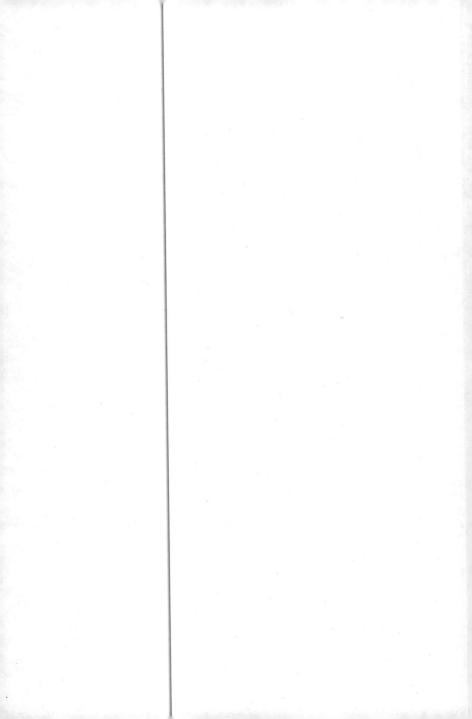

Contents

Introduction
to the Second Edition

IN 2005 CONTINUUM PUBLISHED the first edition of the *Creative Writing MFA Handbook*, and though it's been a short trip since then, it's also been a strange and wonderful one. It was my goal to demystify and illuminate the world of academic creative writing and to what I hope is a helpful extent that goal has been accomplished. Please think of this second edition as part of your toolbox as you venture into the world of MFAs (residency and low-residency) and PhDs. You should also use the other tools at your disposal, including the extensive weblinks in appendix C. This edition, like the first, is not at all intended to be the end word on your choice and path for your graduate degree. But I hope it will get you started on solid footing and then point you in the right direction.

New additions to the *Handbook* include Seth Abramson's outstanding chapter 3, "The Programs." Seth ranks and profiles many of the top programs in the country. I used to be known as the MFA Guru, but it's the truth to say that Seth has taken that title from me. You're in good hands with him. Also, Erika Dreifus and Ed Schwarzschild offer you excellent essays about low-residency MFA and PhD programs in creative writing. Both these areas are outside my experience, so I am especially grateful for Erika's and Ed's expertise, time, and insights. To everyone's pleasure, Adam Johnson returns with "So You've Got an MFA. Now What?"

You may also notice that I've taken away the listings of programs in the back of the book. It seems to me that in this age of the Internet, readers will find much more up-to-date information about MFA program offerings in the links provided in appendix C. As new programs appear, and as established programs change their offerings, the weblinks there will be a better source of information than a book will be. Fear not, however: the listings from the 2006 first edition are available for free on the MFA Blog at http://creative-writing-mfa-handbook.blogspot.com/2008/05/mfa-programs-listing-from-first-edition.html

Meanwhile, the Associated Writing Programs is an organization that supports writers and writing organizations around the world. They publish (for free, now on the Web!) the very helpful AWP Official Guide to Writing Programs (http://guide.awpwriter.org/). Also, Anna Mendoza has the most up-to-date listings of MFA programs, both traditional and low-residency; visit her blogs at http://creativewritingmfa.blogspot.com/ and http://lowresmfa.blogspot.com/

A new acknowledgments section appears in the back of this book, but I would like to note here the much-appreciated support of the following friends, colleagues, and fellow writers: Chellis Ying, Adam Johnson, David Roderick, Stephen Elliott, Scott Hutchins, Eavan Boland, John L'Heureux, Tobias Wolff, Elizabeth Tallent, and Laurie Sandell.

I hope you, the reader, will find this book helpful. You can e-mail me at the MFA blog for any comments or complaints.

Preface

A GRADUATE PROGRAM IN CREATIVE WRITING offers either an MA (Master of Arts, one to two years), an MFA (Master of Fine Arts, two to three years) or a PhD (Doctorate, five or more years) degree where students take writing workshops, craft and literature classes, and work on a book-length thesis of writing. Students explore their writing craft, interact within a community of peers and teachers, and, most important, take advantage of that greatest of gifts: time to write.

There are over one hundred creative writing MFA programs in the United States, over one hundred MA programs with some sort of creative writing emphasis, and a handful, though a growing handful, of creative writing PhD programs. These programs offer degrees primarily in fiction and poetry, though there are a number of universities that offer degrees in creative nonfiction, screenwriting, playwriting, children's literature, and even science writing.

This guide is, first and foremost, a friend of the prospective writing student, and it owes no allegiance to the graduate programs themselves. This guide is intended to be a trustworthy companion as you venture into the intriguing and sometimes intimidating world of what we call the Creative Writing MFA (or MA, or PhD). I offer an overview of programs in general, and a more specific look at some programs in particular. More important, this guide will advise you during the critical stages of your graduate school search: researching, applying, and deciding. I'll answer as many questions as I can, and I'll try to be as definitive as possible.

I want you to think of me as the bus driver. You're on a bus tour in a new city: the city of graduate creative writing programs. I've

lived here for a number of years, and I know my way around. I'm
offering you an introduction to the city and, I hope, a clear, useful,
and entertaining introduction at that. I'll show you the highlights
of this new city, I'll tell you which streets to avoid, I'll offer tips
on how to best spend your time, and I'll even stop the bus a few
times and take a closer look at particular neighborhoods. I've also
brought along some other residents of the city, and they'll offer you
some insights and recommendations as we move along. What I'm
getting at is this: This guide is a starting point, and I intend it to be
a good one. You'll understand the lay of the land once you're done
with your tour. When you're done, I'm encouraging you to get out
there into the city. I'm encouraging you to walk around, find the
best neighborhoods and hot spots that meet your needs. And, I'll
help you figure out what some of those needs are. It's my intention
to get you started right, and equip you with the tools necessary to
make the most of your experience.

So, this is what our tour will involve:

- The Basics. An overview of writing workshops. A breakdown
  of the differences between MA, MFA, and PhD programs.
  I'll talk about low-residency programs, and I'll define all sorts
  of terms like *writing workshop*, *thesis defense*, *studio/academic*,
  secondary language proficiency, and *degree hour*. I'll offer advice
  on where you should "be" in your writing career when applying to graduate programs, and I'll explain the requirements
  of each degree.
- Criteria. To me, this is the most important chapter in the
  book. I want you to think about what you need from a
  creative writing program, because there are definite differences among schools. What sort of funding will you need?
  Would you like to be part of a small writing program or a large
  one? Will you concentrate exclusively on your writing, or do
  you want to take many literature and elective courses? I'll offer
  you a template of what a good writing program looks like, and
  I'll break down each of the criteria—location, funding, teaching, faculty, course work—so that you can decide what you
  need from your graduate experience.
- The Programs. I've profiled fifty creative writing programs.
  Though I strongly encourage you to not limit your search to these,
  this chapter will provide a good starting point for your search.

- The Application Process. Notes on the writing sample, letters of recommendation, the personal statement, the GRE, and the half dozen other aspects of your application. I'll work to keep you organized and on task.
- Decision Time. Once you've applied to programs, you will undoubtedly be accepted and rejected in some combination. When all answers are in, it's time for you to make your decision. The criteria here is a little different from the original search criteria. I'll talk about how to make the best choice for you.
- Overview of the Program and Degree. I'll offer insight into the graduate experience so that you know what to expect, what to take advantage of, and what to avoid. I'll also include special sections on graduate teaching and publishing.
- A wonderful essay by writer Adam Johnson, "So You've Got an MFA. Now What?"
- Links to graduate program reading lists online.
- Helpful Sources. Online and off.
- List of Programs. A complete list of graduate programs, with URL addresses and basic information.

So, before we get the bus rolling out of the lot, a brief introduction is in order. I graduated from the MFA Creative Writing program at the University of Massachusetts in 2001, and afterward I was a Wallace Stegner Fellow in fiction at Stanford University. I currently teach at Stanford. I've been in many, many writing workshops, both as a student and as a teacher. My stories have been published in places like *Best American Non-Required*, *Prairie Schooner*, *Glimmer Train*, and the *San Francisco Chronicle*. At the University of Massachusetts I was the recipient of the Distinguished Teaching Award. I'm thirty-eight years old, and quite frankly, I wish there had been a book like this when I first thought about being a writer. I would have made more of my graduate experience, and I would have avoided some missteps. I have some strong opinions on what makes a good graduate writing program, and you'll definitely hear about them. My goal is to advise and inform. In reverse order.

I expect that this book will cause some controversy in the creative writing community. Though that is not my goal, it is likely unavoidable. Others have strong opinions about their graduate experiences and their graduate schools. I respect those opinions, but I don't have any loyalty to them.

I'm in the prospective student's corner, and not in the corner of the programs themselves. I take my responsibilities as guide (and bus driver) very seriously. I hope this book will be helpful to you, and I hope you'll find some good neighborhoods and avoid some potholes.

In the end, the choice of a writing program, and what you make of the experience, will be yours. This guide offers the information and advice to help make those choices educated, organized, and enlightened.

Very special thanks to the professors, program directors, and current and former students I interviewed for this book—especially George Saunders, Tracy K. Smith, Michael Collier, Heather McHugh, Peter Turchi, Geoffrey Wolff, Aimee Bender, Rachel Kadish, Victoria Chang, Johanna Foster, Maria Hummel, Padma Viswanathan, Scott McCabe, and Bruce Snider. Their very helpful insights and advice appear throughout the book. The opinions expressed outside of their quotes (the rest of the book) are mine alone.

Finally, the acknowledgments section of the book thanks many people, but I'd like to say a special word here to David Roderick and Christina McCarroll who offered insight and very helpful opinions throughout the many stages of this book. Thanks. You two are tops.

All right people. Let's roll on out.

CHAPTER 1

The Basics

I WANT TO BEGIN by simply defining some terms and answering some specific questions.

Why apply to a creative writing program?
This is an important question, and one to which you may already know the answer. I'd like to offer my own answer, though, and I hope you'll keep it in mind throughout your application experience.

People often apply to programs for a variety of reasons: to complete a manuscript, to qualify themselves to teach on the college level, to live and work within a community of writers, and/or to escape back into academia from "the real world." But here's the real reason:

You're drawing a line in the sand, and you're saying *I'm going to be a writer for the next few years, because I've always wanted to do that, and I'm going to see what I can make of myself.* Any reason above and beyond that may actually be a good reason, but that promise to yourself—that you're going to follow your muse and (at my risk of being melodramatic) your dream—is the key to making your experience work for you. If you don't have that, then there are a lot of other options in life, and perhaps you should consider them instead. By choosing the graduate program route, you are staking a claim to being a writer, and you're letting everyone around you know it. Lots of people talk about being a writer; you're doing something about it.

And, of course, on a more practical level you'll be developing your skills as a writer, you'll be studying your craft closely, and you'll be interacting with other students, writing teachers, and lots of good books in order to find your writing voice.

You are buying yourself time. And time is what a writer needs.

So, I need a degree in order to be a writer?

Of course not. If you want to be a writer, write. If you want help along the way, then a graduate program might be a good fit for you.

Keep in mind that a creative writing degree, especially of the MFA variety, is an artistic degree more than it is a professional degree. In this way it is similar to studio art degrees in sculpture, painting, or filmmaking.

Maria Hummel is a Stegner Fellow at Stanford University and a graduate of the MFA program at the University of North Carolina–Greensboro

Q: Why apply to a creative writing program?
A: "One of the most important things I got out of the experience was time. Time to read and write, time to focus on the things I wanted to learn and develop. If you come straight from college, you may not appreciate that time as much, because you've always had it in school. It wasn't until I was out of college for two years that I understood what an incredible luxury it was to have two years of uninterrupted study. Everyone's background is different, but I recommend that people apply to programs when they have a body of interests or experiences that they want to explore through writing."

What are some aspects to a creative writing program?

These can vary of course. But your experience in a program will likely include the class work (writing workshops, literature courses, craft classes, electives), interaction with faculty (in class or sometimes in one-on-one tutorials), attending readings by visiting writers, the completion of a book-length manuscript, and very often your teaching of undergraduates in composition or creative writing classes. Programs may also have community outreach in the form of mentoring high school students or holding public readings by graduate students. Often there are literary magazines connected with the program, where graduate students can gain editorial and publishing experience. And, of course, there is the formal or informal literary community that generally emerges by placing so many writers in one place. The community atmosphere may take the form of readings by graduate students, informal workshops and reading groups, and parties and other social functions. I would expect you to make some friends in your program, many of them lifelong friends and fellow writers. And of course, you'll immerse yourself in reading and writing.

Where should I "be" in my writing career when applying to graduate programs?

Creative writing programs rarely expect your work to have been previously published. MFA programs don't normally require you to have majored in English in your undergraduate work, though some PhD and, to a lesser extent MA, programs may expect this.

Basically, programs expect you to read a lot and write a lot. And this experience needs to be evident in the quality of your writing sample (part of your application, ten to thirty pages of your creative work). I'll emphasize this later, but do keep in mind that your writing sample is, by far, the #1 most important element of your application. If the application readers (normally the professors of the program) like your work, then you have a great chance of being accepted. If they don't like your work, you have no chance.

I won't address the writing sample right now. I want to keep you, and me, on track. I'll address the writing sample and many other aspects in the application section.

Basically, you should be living a life that emphasizes literature and writing. What do I mean by that? Lots of things. If you took creative writing workshops and literature courses in your undergraduate work, then that helps. More important, those classes will give you a feel for what a graduate writing program will be like.

If you've never taken a writing workshop before, let me strongly encourage you to take a class soon. Writing classes are often taught as adult education classes at universities, at community colleges, online through extension courses (UCLA has a highly regarded online extension program), and at local neighborhood and community centers.

Instructors of these classes are often MFA graduates. I'm asking you to take these classes, now, for two reasons:

First, you'll get a clear idea of what your classroom experience will be like in graduate school. That's not to say that workshops aren't different from each other. Depending on the instructor and the other students, the atmosphere can be vastly different. However, the format is generally the same, and you'll know if this type of thing is what you want to be doing for the next two or three years.

Second, if you have little experience in a writing community, you're not likely to get the type of letters of recommendation that can be most helpful for your graduate application. I'll talk more about letters later, but know that a recommendation from a writing teacher who knows your work well is the letter that selection committees will most listen to.

That said, there are many other ways to immerse yourself in your local writing community. Bookstores, libraries, and coffeehouses often hold readings, either of the open-mike variety or of scheduled readers. Pick up a schedule and go to these events. If you live near a university, there are likely to be events there as well. Make a phone call to the English department. Writers' groups are another good way to be thinking and doing something about your writing. Writers' groups have similarities to workshops, but are less formal, and that can often be a good thing. Check your local newspaper or bulletin boards at coffeehouses and cafés.

And of course, read. Read a lot and write a lot. That's the best way to hone your craft. For links to reading lists, including the excellent one developed by the Gotham Writers' Workshop, consult appendix B of this book.

My point in all of this? *Be around* writing, and your writing will improve. And when your writing is improved, you have a better chance of being accepted to graduate programs.

What is the average age of a creative writing graduate student?

That's a good question. There's no data that I'm aware of, but in my nonscientific poll of a dozen former graduate students, the age that came up the most often was twenty-eight. Everyone said there were younger students—straight out of college—and much more experienced students in their thirties and forties. But twenty-eight sounds about right to me, as far as an average goes.

There are definitely fifty-plus-year-olds who are pursuing their craft after many years as professionals and/or parents.

But that brings up a point I'd like to make: I don't think it's wise to apply to graduate programs straight out of undergraduate studies. Why not? It's been my observation that these students tend to burn out without having a break from their academic studies. Other people will tell you, "You've got to have life experience before you write." While I agree with that, I also know that there are many twenty-year-olds have much greater life experiences than some fifty-year-olds. That said, taking a break from academia to work, travel, volunteer, teach, or whatever you want, is highly recommended. At the very least, time away from school will help you appreciate the benefits of the academic world. A two-year break between undergraduate and graduate seems sufficient and wise to me.

What is a writing workshop?

The writing workshop is the backbone of any creative writing program. Students generally take four workshops in their concentration (fiction, poetry, nonfiction, etc.). A typical workshop holds ten to sixteen graduate students and one professor. Most workshops will meet once a week, but in some programs workshops meet twice a week. Students turn in poems and stories, the rest of the class reads them, and during the following class "workshop" happens. Basically, the writer remains silent while the class discusses the work in detail. In other words, the writer gets to sit in while the class holds an editorial-type meeting about the work. (Generally, the class will sit around one large table). Questions that might arise are: What are the strengths of this work? What ground is it covering? What were we confused about in the work? What suggestions do we have for improving it? What was our reaction to the work in general and to the voice in particular?

At the end of the workshop, the writer is often allowed to ask questions of the class, either to clarify what has been already said or to cover territory that was not yet discussed. A workshop for a fifteen-page story might last around thirty to forty minutes. The workshop for a one-page poem will last around ten minutes. Obviously, poetry workshops cover more submissions per class.

I'll discuss workshops in greater detail in a later chapter of this book, but for now consider that workshops are an opportunity to hear the reactions and opinions of your readers. It's an opportunity to have some of your assumptions reinforced and other assumptions challenged. You'll get another "take" on your writing, and through that process you can work to improve it. Perhaps most important, workshops provide a way to identify key readers—people who understand what you are trying to do and who can help you achieve it—that you can lean on during your graduate experience and throughout your writing life.

What do you mean when you say "literature" course?

I mean classes where you'll study books, write papers about them, and discuss them in class. There are also "craft" classes, which are a type of literature class, but focused more closely on the writer's perspective. For example, a literature class studying Virginia Woolf's *Mrs. Dalloway* may focus on the time period, social norms, historical events, gender and class issues, and linguistic influences that impacted the book. Meanwhile, a craft class studying the same book might focus on the choices and techniques Woolf uses to construct the language and narrative. Many literature classes are blends of craft classes, and in many craft classes students will work on imitations (writing in the voice of the author) or other writing assignments (with a focus, say, on voice, form, narration, dialogue, or description).

Obviously, literature and craft classes can vary depending on the instructor and the program, and on the students for that matter. But the important distinction to remember is that a workshop class will focus on in-progress student writing, while a literature/craft class will focus on published writing. But some of the best and most innovative workshops and literature classes will include aspects of each other.

What are the requirements of a graduate degree?

These will vary from program to program, but generally the requirements will include writing workshops, literature classes, electives, a book-length thesis, and a defense of that thesis before a committee. Some programs require proficiency in a secondary language, and others require a reading list and graduate exam. I'll address the three types of degrees here in *very* general terms:

MA degree—Master of Arts. One to two years. Six to twelve classes. About a 3:1 ratio between literature classes and writing workshops. A master's exam on a specific reading list is almost always required, as is a final creative thesis. A secondary language proficiency is often required. Most MA degrees concentrate on the study of literature first and the crafting of writing second, so it's an appropriate degree for students who want to immerse themselves in literature but who still want to write creatively.

MFA degree—Master of Fine Arts. Two to three years. Eight to sixteen classes. Four writing workshops are almost always required, as are about an equal number of literature courses. Many programs offer classes in the craft of writing, and other programs encourage students to take electives in other departments such as art, psychology, history, and others. A creative thesis (book length) is always required, as is its defense in front of a committee. A secondary language and a master's exam in literature may be required, but not often. This is an appropriate degree for students who wish to focus primarily on their own writing, with secondary emphasis on literature and other classes.

PhD degree—Doctor of Philosophy. Five or more years. Ten to eighteen classes. Two advanced exams (one written, one oral) related to reading lists are normally required, as is a secondary language proficiency, and a final creative dissertation and its defense. Generally speaking, this is a PhD degree in English with a secondary emphasis in creative writing. Many PhD programs will accept credits that students earned during their MA or MFA study. This is an appropriate degree for students who want to study literature at an advanced, intensive level, and who wish to work on their own writing for some of that time.

Do these vary from program to program?
Yes, very much so. Some MFA degrees in creative writing may actually lean more toward the literature side, as opposed to the creative writing side. Meanwhile, there are some PhD and MA programs that concentrate primarily on writing. The bottom line: A program's list of requirements and classes will give you a clear sense of the emphasis of the degree.

I'll give you a rule of thumb: Something close to a 2:1 or 1:1 ratio of literature and writing workshops is a program concentrating on creative writing. Something closer to a 3:1 ratio or higher is a program concentrating in literature.

Keep in mind that programs that offer a fair number of electives (two or more) offer students the best flexibility, because students can choose their own concentration: literature, writing classes, or classes outside the English department.

Are there other terms for these concentrations?
Yes. They are "studio" for concentrations in writing and craft classes, and "academic" for writing degrees concentrating in literature. And of course, there is the hybrid "studio/academic." These terms are not often used, but from time to time you'll see them on a program's website. Now you know what they mean.

What is a degree hour?
That's easy. Sort of.

One class generally equals three degree hours. In other words, a twenty-four-hour master's degree will equal eight classes. However, it does get tricky: often "thesis hours" are given for work on the longer writing project and sometimes workshops and nonworkshop classes will count as six degree hours. Bottom line: Be clear about how many total *classes* a program requires, rather than how many degree hours.

Can you, like, give me an example of a program's requirements, so I know what you're talking about?
Sure. Let's take a quick trip to the University of Michigan's website. It's available at http://www.lsa.umich.edu/english/grad/mfa/.

The University of Michigan is a two-year MFA program in fiction or poetry. The program is thirty-six degree hours, and in this case that means four workshops, four literature classes, plus thesis hours (work toward your book-length manuscript). The website indicates that there is some flexibility in changing one literature class to a class outside the department. A secondary language proficiency is required, as is a final thesis.

My conclusion, therefore, (based on the 1:1 ratio) is that the program concentrates on the writing aspect, as opposed to primarily on the literature aspect. As an aside, I like the flexibility that the program offers in choosing your classes.

What is a thesis defense?
Oh man, we are getting off track here. Quickly: Not all programs will required a thesis defense, but I think it's an important aspect to a program. You write a collection of stories or poems (or a novel, screenplay, play, etc.). A fiction/nonfiction thesis will be 120 pages

or more. A poetry thesis will be 40 pages or more. You choose a committee of three professors to read it, then you "defend" it in a thesis meeting. Basically, you'll be asked questions about your literary vision, voice, decisions, and goals. Some people are intimidated by this process, but I don't think it is necessary to be. Check it out: One of those committee members will be your adviser. And your adviser will tell you when your manuscript is ready to be defended. I've often heard of students who have had to rework their manuscripts on the advice of the adviser (before the defense; this might take an extra semester). But I've rarely heard of a student who fails his or her thesis defense. Generally speaking, the purpose of the committee and defense is to challenge and encourage (in some combination or another) your overall creative graduate work.

Many programs will use only a thesis adviser, and not a committee, and that may work out just fine.

However, if a program does not require a thesis at all, then that's a program not particularly interested in your work.

Do most programs require a secondary language proficiency?
Almost all PhD programs will require a secondary language proficiency, and so will many MA programs. As for the MFA programs, I'd say that about 20 percent require a secondary language proficiency. Proficiency might be measured in the form of an exam, course work, or translation. If you wish to learn or continue your study in a secondary language at a program that does not require it, my guess is that you can use your electives to take language and translation classes.

When you say PhD, MFA, and MA programs in this book, do you always mean creative writing programs (or programs that have an emphasis in creative writing), or do you sometimes mean programs in English or other subjects?
I always mean creative writing programs. If I mean another subject, including English with no creative writing aspect, then I'll indicate it.

What is a low-residency program?
Outstanding question. Low-residency programs are a small but quickly expanding type of program. They are almost exclusively MFA programs.

Low-residency programs are a type of distance-learning degree in creative writing. You don't have to be present at the university full-time in order to obtain a degree.

I really like the idea behind low-residency programs, as they allow a great flexibility for students who have family or career responsibilities where they currently live. Here's how they work: Generally speaking, a student is matched with a teacher for a semester. The student receives a reading list from the teacher, and the student also sends stories or poems, and revisions of these stories and poems, to the teacher throughout the semester. The teacher sends back comments and suggestions. It's basically a long-distance one-on-one workshop. Communication may be through e-mail, post, or phone, depending on the teacher's preference. Classes are not necessarily limited to the "workshop" type, and literature classes may be offered. Either way, there is an expanding reading list that the student must complete and report on.

In most cases, each semester will begin with a seven- to ten-day conference, where *all* of the students and *all* of the teachers actually do attend the university and hold workshops, seminars, and classes. Sometimes these conferences take place over the summer. In any case, these events are intensive, required for the degree, and from what I've heard, a lot of fun.

The upsides to low-residency programs are that they offer great time flexibility (a degree can be completed over the course of a few or many years), and they offer great one-on-one relationships with other writers. The two biggest downsides are (1) there is less of a "visible" community of writers, though there is a community in its own way, especially during the conferences and (2) very rarely is there funding available for students. Students pay their way through the course of the program. A four-semester low-residency course of study will cost $20,000 or more.

Either way, low-residency programs are excellent options for students who wish to concentrate on their writing without moving to a new location.

Rachel Kadish teaches in the Lesley University MFA program. Her work includes *From a Sealed Room* and *Soon also for You*.

Q: From a teacher's perspective, how does the low-residency format work?
A: "I don't know whether writing can be taught, but I believe it can be coached, like athletics can be coached. I'll stand on my head for my students, but they've got to run the laps themselves. What I love about the low-residency setup is that I meet with each student. They tell me what they need as a writer, and I'll tell them was I observe. We agree on what they will read. They do craft annotations. I focus on different things for different students. They read this novel or these short stories. It's very individualized, and you can see a real blossoming during the course of a semester. I encourage students to pay close attention to what interests them. You can see a big change in just a few months."

Scott McCabe is a recent graduate of the Lesley University MFA program:

Q: What advice would you offer students who are considering the low-residency format?
A: "What's important is really considering the nature of the programs themselves. You have to be realistic about how much self-teaching goes into it. There are an entirely different set of benefits and problems that go along with this kind of program. You get to know your teachers extremely well. The mentoring aspect is very strong. On the other hand, you're disconnected from your peers for much of the year. It takes more to stay motivated. At the same time, it's good preparation for the actual life of a writer. Students should understand both sides of the experience."

Are there masters programs in creative writing outside the United States?

Yes, there are. I've included a list of some of them in appendix D. Detailed information is difficult to find for many of these programs, but the best resource for information is available at http://www. gradschools.com/listings/out/creative_write_out.html. Countries listed include Mexico, England, Ireland, Scotland, Spain, Australia, New Zealand, Norway, the Philippines, and South Korea. The site holds basic information, plus e-mail contact addresses.

What can you tell me about funding?

I can tell you a lot, and most of what I'll tell you will be in the next chapter. That said, a sneak preview is this: In my opinion (and the opinion of most writers and graduate students) funding from the program is critical to your graduate experience. Many programs offer funding to students in the form of writing fellowships and teaching assistantships. In these cases, your tuition is waived and you receive a stipend of anywhere from $5,000 to $15,000.

I'd say that about 20 percent of programs fund *all or most* of their students. Another 40 percent fund *some* of their students, and the remaining 40 percent fund *only a few or none* of their students. The discrepancy in funding has more to do with resources than anything else. Most graduate students in other fields pay for their graduate study. That said, a program with resources—financial and otherwise—is a program you want.

Keep in mind that a year's tuition at a private school may be upwards of $30,000, while tuition at a public in-state school may be only $4,000. And there is everything in between. Needless to say, a tuition waiver goes a long way.

You know better than I do about your funding needs. If you are independently wealthy, then you've got a lot of options. Otherwise, a basic principle of this book is to encourage students to seek programs that offer funding. If funding is not available, I'm encouraging students to aim their sites at *affordable* programs rather than expensive ones. More about that in the next chapter. And in every chapter for that matter.

What will be included in my application packet, and are we back on track now?

Yes, we've been back on track for the last couple of questions. Thanks for asking.

Sorry to keep saying, "More on this later, here's a quick preview," but I want this chapter to be an overview and subsequent chapters to dive in to specifics.

Application requirements may vary. But generally speaking, an MFA program will require a writing sample (about twenty-five pages of prose or fifteen of poetry), three letters of recommendation, a personal statement, undergraduate transcripts, GRE scores, and the application form itself. Some MFA programs will require a critical essay in some form.

For PhD programs and some MA programs add to that list the GRE literature subject scores and definitely the critical essay.

My bet is that no two of your potential programs will ask for the same materials in the same order, so keeping track of all of these elements is essential.

Bruce Snider is a former Wallace Stegner Fellow at Stanford University and a James A. Michener Fellow at the University of Texas. His works include _The Year We Studied Women_, winner of the Felix Pollak Prize in Poetry.

Q: How many programs should students apply to?
A: "Well, I think a lot. As many as you can afford to apply to. I applied to ten or twelve. That was a pretty good number. So much of the admissions process is subjective. You want to increase the chances of your work finding a sympathetic reader. The more applications you put out there the more likely you are to get into a program with funding, in a place you'd like to live."

How many programs will I be applying to?

Why beat around the bush here? You'll apply to eight to twelve programs. Why? Because I said so. And because, for the most part, you can't predict who will like your writing sample and who will not. And if you apply to three programs and none of those readers likes your writing sample, then you have no options. Instead, spread your net wide. Keep your options open. I can tell you this: I applied to five schools, and when I got rejected to the first three and waitlisted for the fourth, I definitely wish I'd applied to more. Don't be a dummy like me.

Keep in mind that the application fee for each school will be $40–55. Sure, that adds up, but hey, this is your life here. Make the investment in yourself.

When are the deadlines for applications?
They begin in the beginning of December and go as late as mid-February. Make sure you know the deadlines for your particular schools and stick to them. The vast majority of deadlines will fall in January.

How do I choose my best writing sample?
Sorry. No preview on that. See chapter 4.

What criteria should I use for selecting programs where I'll apply?
All right, a very short preview on this. The next chapter is focused almost exclusively on this question.

In order: (1) location (where will you live, work, and grow during these years?); (2) funding (will you receive funding or will you pay for your graduate education?); (3) teaching opportunities (is this important to you, and if so, what sort of opportunities for teaching are available to you?); (4) faculty (who will you be working with during your years in the program?); (5) other aspects, including program size and degree flexibility.

That's a lot of information in one chapter. Can we get a summary?
No problem.

Chapter Summary

1. There are many reasons to apply to a creative writing program, but the main reason is to provide yourself the time and space to actually *be* a writer instead of simply hoping to be one. Other reasons include teaching experience, the writing community, and, of course, developing your skills as a writer.

2. The three types of degrees are the MA, the MFA, and the PhD. There are more than one hundred MA programs in the

United States and over a hundred MFA programs. There are about two dozen PhD programs with emphases in creative writing. An MA program is generally one to two years. An MFA is generally two to three years, and a PhD is five years or more. All programs will include some form of course work (writing workshops, literature classes, craft classes, and electives), interaction with faculty, readings by visiting writers, the completion of a book-length manuscript (and its defense in front of a committee), and very likely some form of teaching. Other aspects may include community outreach, a final graduate exam and reading list, a secondary language proficiency, working on the editorial board of a literary magazine, and public readings.

3. Low-residency programs are a good fit if you have a full-time job you intend to keep, or if you cannot travel to another location for family or career reasons. Most low-residency programs require two annual ten-day residencies on campus with faculty and other students, and then the rest of the year students are matched one-on-one with writing teachers who direct their study through e-mail or mail correspondence.

4. Workshops are the backbone of creative writing programs. They offer writers a chance to hear reactions and suggestions about their work from a class of their peers and teachers. Literature classes, craft classes, and electives make up the remainder of the course work.

5. An application to a creative writing program will include some combination of a writing sample, three letters of recommendation, a personal statement, undergraduate transcripts, GRE scores, and in some cases a critical essay and GRE subject scores.

6. Potential students should apply to eight to twelve schools, and funding should be a top priority when researching programs.

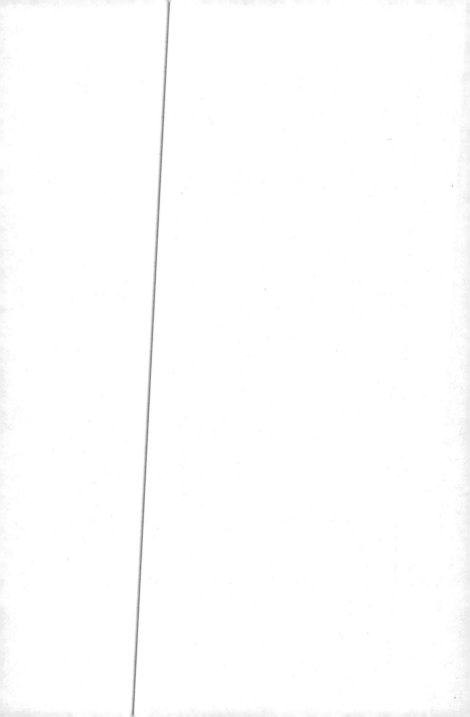

CHAPTER 2

What to Look For in a
Creative Writing Program

THE BEST CREATIVE WRITING PROGRAMS have good support—financial and otherwise—for their graduate students, and they provide a variety of opportunities in the classroom, in teaching experience, and in publishing. I've listed below what I consider to be the most important elements of a solid creative writing program. I'd doubt that any one program will get high marks on *all* of these aspects, but do keep these things in mind. A solid program will provide most of these opportunities. Some aspects may be more important to you than others, and some of them might not be relevant if for example, you're seeking a low-residency MFA. In any case, I'd encourage you to create your own list of "must haves" when you're making your initial and final selections.

Financial Support. A solid residential program provides full funding for most, if not all, its graduate students in the form of fellowships, teaching assistantships, editing and research assistantships, and scholarships. Programs that fund all of their students are in the minority, but at the very least programs should have affordable tuition and should seek additional funding sources for their students.

Teaching Experience. The program should provide an opportunity for graduate students to teach at least one year of college or creative writing.

Faculty. An acceptable teacher/student ratio is 1:12. Lower is better of course. Faculty should have consistent publications and a consistent record of teaching excellence. You can easily find a list of faculty publications by searching the Web. A measure of teaching excellence is best discovered by speaking with current students in the program, but I'll encourage you to hold off on that until you are actually accepted to the program. Students are much more likely to spend time with you then, and the idea of "teaching excellence" is more important to your final decision than it is to your preliminary list of programs.

Class Size. The best workshop size is ten to twelve graduate students.

Literary Magazines and Presses. The existence of a literary magazine connected with the school or program (and/or a small university press) will likely provide editorial experience and internships. A healthy writing program is connected to the writing field outside the university.

Visiting Writers. A clear list of visiting writers should be available on the program's website. A program that brings three to four visiting writers a year, or more, is the sign of a financially healthy program. Big names are good, though some rising stars are more likely to visit classrooms and give students some face time.

Community Outreach. At the University of Massachusetts we had a program through the Writers in Schools organization where MFA students visited classrooms in local high schools. This was terrific experience, and a lot of fun, and it showed that the program had a good reputation in the community. Other community outreach could include programs for the elderly, prisons, writer's groups, and youth societies.

Graduate Student Readings. To me, this is a real key for judging how serious the program takes its graduate students. When I lived in North Carolina, I'd often attend the UNCG MFA program thesis readings. One poet and one fiction writer (both MFA students) would hold readings, sponsored by the university in their final year of the program. It was a big deal. Lots of undergraduates, faculty, and often the MFA students' parents (flying in from the other side of the country) would attend. It was very clear that the graduate students were highly valued by the program. Meanwhile, at UMass–Amherst, we were left to create a reading series on our own at a local bookstore. That was actually a lot of fun, but hey, a program could do *both*. In any case, a strong graduate student reading series—on or off campus—gets high marks from me. It shows that a program is committed to, and celebrates and values, its students and their creative work.

Contacts with Editors and Agents. This sounds like a big thing, and yes, it can be a big thing. But it's not likely to be promoted on a program's website. This is another question to ask current students. Formal or informal seminars about magazine publishing and the business of writing (offered by faculty or visitors) is another sign of a solid program.

Student Publications. If current or previous graduate students are publishing books and in magazines, then the website should be highlighting this information. This is another big key for me. While publication does not necessarily equate with excellence, a program should be interested in promoting its students' creative work.

Courses within the Department. A list of graduate classes should be available from the website. (If not, then do contact the program coordinator.) A solid list of literature classes is always a good thing. Classes aimed specifically at writers is even better. Classes about publishing and editing are terrific signs for a program.

Courses outside the Department. Some flexibility in attending classes outside the department, I think, is an important element of a graduate student experience. Two "flexible" classes (six degree hours, normally) is about right.

Graduating Students. The program should graduate a high number of its incoming students. Keep in mind that creative writers are a fickle group. Some arrive at a program and decide that the *life*, not necessarily the program, is not right for them. An 85% graduation rate is acceptable. Anything lower is not necessarily a deal breaker, but it's a question you should explore with current students. The program coordinator should have these statistics. If he or she doesn't, then ask to be referred to the right person at the graduate school. Again, this is something you should consider during your final choice.

The Library. A well-stocked university library is always a good thing. A program-specific library, like the excellent one at the University of Virginia, is an even better sign that the program takes its students research and reading seriously. Often programs will have their holdings in the main library.

Graduate Student Representation on Committees. I'm not talking about thesis committees, which I'll discuss next. I'm talking about committees that help plan and coordinate the program's yearly events, visitors, and functions. I'm also talking about graduate student representation on committees that set long-term goals for the program. To me, this is a real key for determining how seriously a program takes its students. I certainly don't expect a graduate student to be put in charge of the budget. (Ha!) But a program that doesn't get input from its graduate students is a program completely out of touch with its biggest population. Noy Holland, at UMass, often placed students on program committees, and they offered good insight in to the needs and contributions of the graduate population. A solid program has two or three student representatives on a variety of planning committees. This type of information is not likely available on the website, though it *should* be. Ask the program coordinator about student representation.

The Thesis. A final thesis is often required for graduation. The thesis consists of the student's chosen creative work from his or her time at the institution. Basically, it's a book, or part of a book, of creative work. A solid program always requires a thesis. Some programs will call this something else (a project, a manuscript, etc.), and that's fine. Bottom line: One adviser and perhaps a small committee of faculty should be reading and giving feedback (criticism and encouragement) about the student's completed work. A program that does not require a final thesis is a program that is not very interested in the career of the student.

Final Note: I want to reiterate here: It's likely that no program has *all* of these elements. But the best programs will have most of them. Keep them in mind as a checklist, and as a measurement, for your future program.

Chapter Summary

1. You've got to be kidding me. Do you know how short this chapter is?

2. Oh, all right. A solid graduate program in creative writing provides funding for the majority of its students, teaching experience, a well-regarded faculty, and good class sizes (ten to twelve) and student-to-teacher ratio (12:1 or lower). Literary magazines and presses are helpful to a program and its students, as are community outreach and an impressive visiting writers series. A graduate student reading series is a good sign of a solid program, as is a required thesis, and so is student representation on planning committees. A course list with a variety of classes is a must, as is a little flexibility in taking classes outside the department. Contacts with editors and agents, a strong record of publication from past graduates, and a high graduation rate (85 percent or higher) are all signs of an impressive program.

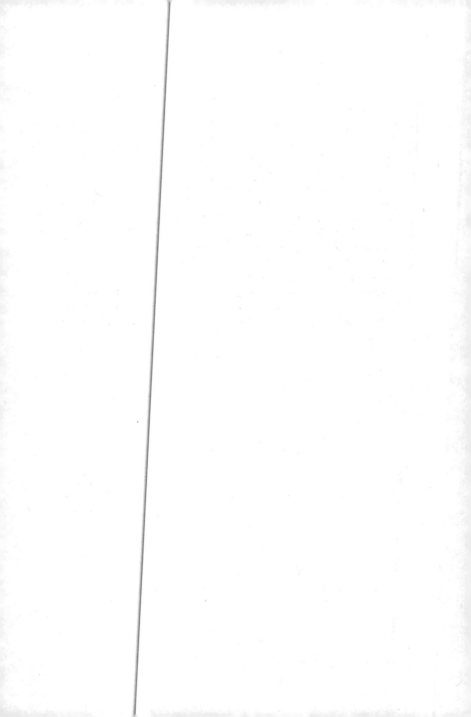

CHAPTER 2A

Criteria

BY THE END OF THIS CHAPTER you should understand what criteria you will use to select your programs, and you should also know where to go to find the information you need about the individual schools.

For the most part, you'll find information about the particular programs on their universities' websites. Appendix C lists resources for finding programs. Keep in mind that information can change from year to year, and so it's in your best interests to consult the program websites.

One note on the websites: In my opinion, a poorly designed website indicates a poorly designed creative writing program. This is the twenty-first century. Program directors should be seeking the best applicants by making their information clear and accessible. A good website need not be flashy or filled with bells and whistles. But the information prospective students are seeking—about faculty, funding, curriculum, and the like should be clear and straightforward. A phone number and e-mail contact should also be readily available.

What sort of criteria should I use in selecting and applying to programs?
I'm going to swim directly against the tide of conventional wisdom about how to select the program that is right for you. Most articles and advice about programs have centered on faculty, encouraging prospective students to seek out the best faculty writers and to choose their program in accordance with this. What is not often mentioned, but what should be obvious, is that the "best" writers

don't often make the best teachers. Certainly, sometimes they do, but often the biggest name writers in a program teach only one class a year. Keep in mind that professors can be on sabbatical, and even more often, they move from program to program, so the faculty you begin with may not be the faculty you end with. It simply doesn't make sense to me to make a two- to three-year life choice based primarily on the faculty criteria. So, while most advice is to place faculty first in your decision, I am strongly encouraging you to place it about fourth.

So what's the first criteria then?

Hold on. I first want to state the obvious, in case it is not so for some prospective students. In many ways, you'll first focus your search based on your genre. If you're interested in fiction or poetry, then you have hundreds of options. If creative nonfiction is your interest, there are dozens of programs that can accommodate you. Screenwriting, playwriting, children's literature, and other genres are much more limited. So, keep this in mind. I'm not counting it as a criteria to explore, because I'm assuming you already know your genre.

Okay. So what's the first criteria?

Location. Where do you want to live? Where will you be most comfortable and challenged as a writer? You'll spend the majority of your time in the program *alone*, writing. Make sure your environment is one that you like, and one that you can build a life within. Do you want to live in a big city or a small town? Do you want to live on one of the coasts and, if so, which one? Do you need lots of sunshine, or snow, or nightlife, or nature? Considering these questions first and foremost will help narrow your search from a hundred programs to a more manageable number.

And, I offer some cautionary advice: Definitely make a list of the places you want to live, but also make a list of, as writer Steve Almond says, "the places where you *could stand* to live." Though I think location is the most important initial criteria, it's not the only one. Keep your needs in mind, but also keep your options open.

I thought you said funding was important. Where does that fit on the list?

It's right here, at number two. Keep in mind: You're narrowing your list of potential programs, not making your final selection.

Funding might be number one on your list as you make your final decision on where to attend.

That said, how much do you want to pay for your creative writing degree? If you are independently wealthy, then perhaps Columbia—a university with an outstanding reputation—is the right one for you. At $33,000 a year, with little chance for a fellowship or tuition waiver, you'll be $66,000 in the hole after two years, and since some students stay for three, you might be as much as $100,000 in the hole. Plus the expenses of living in New York City.

Well, you can see what my attitude is toward these type of programs. I don't like schools that charge exorbitant amounts to study writing. Why not? First of all, there are many other schools that do offer funding, or who offer affordable tuition. Second, if you're going to be a writer you should get in the habit of living cheaply, at least till you sell a few books, which may be a number of years away. And third, and very important in my mind, is that expensive programs tend to have less diverse workshops. I'm not talking particularly about racial diversity or gender diversity, I'm talking about life diversity. People from many different parts of the country and the world who have had different experiences to share within the workshop. In many ways, I am talking about economic diversity.

As Johanna Foster, a potential MFA student, points out, a program that charges very high tuition is likely to get three kinds of students, "The rich, the very rich, and the financially irresponsible." And that's not to say that these three groups might not have much to offer a workshop, it's just that there's no sense in limiting your peers to these three groups.

Why do programs charge tuition?

Most graduate students outside of creative writing pay in full for their education. Running a university and running a program require money. Much of this money comes from tuition, though many programs are funded through a combination of donors and grants. Many schools fund their students through teaching assistantships, where graduate students teach composition and creative writing to undergraduates.

My point: There are funding options out there. You may end up paying tuition for your creative writing education, and that's fine. But make sure it's affordable to your budget, and before you pay, explore your options.

What about programs that fund some students and don't fund others?

These programs are limited financially, as are most graduate programs in a variety of fields. Education costs money. The tuition of some students pays for the existence of the program.

That said, I want to caution you about what I'll call "tiered" funding. Tiered funding offers fellowships for writing, teaching, or research to *some* students and requires tuition from other students. Again, this is a necessity for many programs. However, I'm concerned about the competitive atmosphere that arises in some of these programs.

For example, let's take the State College of Nowhere. This university accepts thirty students each year. Ten students are fully funded through writing and teaching fellowships, ten students are partially funded through the same means (a half-tuition waiver, or a stipend that covers three-quarters, a half, or a quarter of tuition), and ten students pay full tuition and fees.

So, who determines who gets the ten full fellowships? The program director chooses, with perhaps some input from the other professors.

This is fine if you're in the top funding third, but there's a catch: There is sometimes a "reranking" of students in the second year. So while you may start out in the top third, you may end up partially funded in the second year, or paying full tuition. How are these rerankings determined? That's hard to say, and even program directors (who, again, are often forced to make these decisions because of budgetary constraints) might not be able to say. What we hear most is "potential as a writer." And what is that based on? Lots of things: The quality of your writing in workshop, your ability to get your work published in magazines, your ability as a student, and very likely your ability to network with and influence the people in a position to make these choices.

My point? Programs that are forced to "tier" the funding of their students often create very competitive atmospheres and relationships between their graduate students. For example, if you're in the running for one of the top spots, what kind of workshop critiques will you offer students who you are competing with? What will you say about their work in the presence of faculty members (who will be ranking the students at the end of the year)? What will other students say about your work? Will you be likely to offer your time and friendship to people who you are in direct competition with? Will they offer you this time and friendship?

In a perfect world, perhaps. Keep in mind that as a writer you are in competition with yourself. You are always trying to improve your craft and voice. You shouldn't spend time worrying whether you're a "better" writer than your colleagues. "Better" is subjective, and writers are different rather than "better" or "worse." However, I want you to keep this competitive funding atmosphere in mind. I don't see that it is helpful for most writers, though it may be unavoidable for many programs.

Am I clear? When you're narrowing your initial choices, do some "tiering" of your own. Fully funded programs first, partially funded programs second, and low-funded programs last.

Are there other forms of financial aid?

Yes. There are loans, some university-wide grants, and, of course, there is in-state tuition. If you end up attending a public university, you should plan on taking the steps to become a resident as soon as you are accepted. You should also fill out the FASA (the Free Application for Federal Student Aid), which will greatly help your eligibility for a variety of funding sources. For the most part, the majority of the available funding will come directly through the creative writing program or the English department.

Do look at appendix B for information on the FASA and also the Jacob Javits Fellowship.

Do tuition and fees vary greatly among programs?

Oh, yes. Obviously, tuition will be higher at private colleges and sometimes significantly lower at public institutions. Tuition is lower if you are a resident of a particular state. Do keep in mind that you can gain residency in a short or long period of time, depending on the state.

I think it's a very good idea to lean toward public universities if finances will be an issue for you.

I'm confused now, and discouraged.

I'm sorry. I didn't mean to discourage or confuse anyone, least of all you. Let me be clear: Around 20 percent of programs fund all or most of their graduate students. Around 40 percent fund most or some of their graduate students. And around 40 percent of programs fund some or none of their students. Obviously some creative writing graduate students in the country will be funded, and others will not. The tuition at public universities is more affordable than that at private universities. I'm asking you to keep your financial needs in mind, and to rank your schools accordingly.

In the next chapter I'll profile around fifty programs, and I'll be as clear as I can about funding. In the meantime, you can get a very good feel for the funding level of a program by visiting its website. Look under *tuition, financial aid*, or *fellowships*. If a school offers funding to the majority of its students, then the website will state this. If the program does not offer funding at all, or if it has a clear-cut "tiered" system, then it will likely be vague about funding. I'm encouraging you to lean toward the programs that state their funding information clearly.

Do you feel better now?

A little. Thanks.
No problem.

So, location is first, and funding is second. What's third?
Third is teaching. I'm a big fan of acquiring teaching experience during your graduate program years. It's essential if you plan on teaching after the program, and even if you're not planning on teaching later you still learn a lot from your students. I think Thomas E. Kennedy puts it best: "There is no doubt that teaching is the best way to learn because it forces you to test your assumptions and see if they're really true."

It's my opinion that you don't really understand a subject completely until you have to teach it to others.

In my first creative writing class I remember telling students that it's more important for your characters to be vulnerable rather than tough. Why? Because in real life we certainly like our friends and family members because of their strengths, but we also love them for their weaknesses as well. It's both, and you can ask any parent that. Meanwhile, on the page, we like characters who make mistakes, who use bad judgment, who say the wrong things, and we also like it when they work their way out of these situations. Or work their way deeper into a hole. In any case, I remember saying this, and I can remember a student, Sylvie, who asked, "Well, *how* do you make your characters vulnerable?"

A good question, and one I did not have the answer to. It's one thing to make a statement, and it's another thing to prove it and show it, which is what teaching is much about. For the next class I brought in an excerpt from "The Point" by Charles D'Ambrosio. It's about a boy, thirteen years old, who guides drunk adults along a beach at night so that they don't fall in the water and drown. It's actually about much more than that, but for the purpose of this little aside, let's leave it at that. The boy, Kurt, is smart, he's capable, he's focused, he thinks these adults are ridiculous, but he's very serious about his job and he does it better than anyone in the world. A tough kid. While his adult companions are sobbing drunk about their failed marriages, their poor financial investments, their distant relationships with their children, Kurt's response is always, "There's time to think about that tomorrow. For now, let's just get you home."

But there's this wonderful moment near the middle of the story when Kurt relates to the reader his theory of "The Black Hole." The black hole is, like the imploded star in space, a great vacuum in your life, and it's constantly pulling on you, drawing you in, trying to suck the life out of you. His father, he feels, fell into this black hole the year before. "He shot himself in the head one morning—did I already say this?" he relates to us. And later, "You understand, I miss Father, miss having him around to tell me what's right and what's wrong, or to talk about boom-boom, which is sex, or just to go salmon fishing out by Hat Island and not worry about things." Suddenly, at these moments, the story opens up and breathes for us. We see some things very clearly, not the least of which is that Kurt feels an enormous guilt for allowing his father to fall into his depression, into his black hole, and Kurt's job, guiding these often ridiculous drunks home, is a way to make amends for this. It's touching, at least to me, because there's no reason a thirteen-year-old should have to feel guilty about being a poor "guide" to adults, and yet Kurt feels this clearly and deeply.

In any case, we talked about this in class, I pointed out some things I could see, and students pointed out some things I never would have. I knew it was important to make your characters vulnerable, but I only had the slightest knowledge of how to actually *do* it, on the page. I'm not saying I'm an expert now, but I'm closer thanks to that particular student's question, and thanks to my own work in thinking about it before class.

So, I think teaching is very helpful to a writer, and I'd encourage you to seek out these opportunities in your graduate program. I taught composition long before I taught creative writing, and I learned much from my students and myself during this time as well.

My point? If you want to improve your writing, and increase your chances of funding, and gain experience in teaching, then keep your eye on programs that offer opportunities for teaching assistantships.

And by the way, assistantships vary. You may be in charge of a class. You may be assisting a professor with a larger class. Both have their advantages.

But if I teach, I'll have less time for my writing.
True. And not true. Teaching takes time away from your writing. Teaching can take up a lot of time. One class, especially during your first semester (when you're figuring things out), can take up twenty to twenty-five hours a week in grading, preparing, commenting, and all the other things that go along with running a classroom.

On the other hand, for some people, if you are forced to be organized in the classroom, you'll learn skills about being organized in your writing time. When I'm busy teaching, it takes away from my writing time. Conversely, when I'm teaching, I'm excited about writing, and I make the most of the free time that I *do* have.

I'm going to avoid becoming tedious here. You either want the teaching experience—or rather, the experience of teaching—or you want the time. I'm ranking teaching third. Consider it in your own way, and rank it accordingly.

I sense that you want to get off this subject, but at the same time, you don't *really* want to get off this subject.
Ah, you are the master of intuition and observation. You will make a wonderful writer.

Keep in mind some programs will want you to teach from the first semester. Others, the second year. Meanwhile, some programs would like you to teach two or three classes a semester, and I would encourage you to stay *well away* from these programs. These graduate students are more indentured servants than writers in training.

I really think highly of teaching experience. I became a better writer in trying to improve the writing of others. Teaching brings me energy and insight, and if you feel like it will do the same for you, keep this aspect high on your list of criteria.

Feel better?
Yep.

Are there other types of assistantships?
Yes. There are also research assistantships, where you do, well, research on behalf of a professor on a particular topic. This can be very rewarding and can teach you a lot of skills. They also pay, usually quite well for the hours involved. Editorial assistantships are also often available if the university has a literary magazine or small press.

Last thoughts on assistantships?
Be sure to find information about assistantships on the program's website. Often, the application for these positions is separate from the actual graduate application. They are also often required *after* you've been accepted, and not before.

So, decide whether or not you'll want to teach or research or not. Aim at programs that offer your preference. (And decide whether there are enough positions to go around. The website should indicate a number or a percentage.) Teaching is actually part of funding, though teaching is more than funding, so I list it separately.

Can you summarize where we are right now?
These top three criteria—location, funding, and teaching—are the main criteria for most students, at least in their initial research stage. If you don't care where you live, and you don't need funding, and you don't care to teach, then you'll move the following criteria way up. Otherwise, you will have narrowed your search of hundreds of schools down to about twenty or thirty, or fewer in some cases, based on these top three criteria.

Okay, what's the fourth criteria?
Faculty is the fourth criteria.

Good teachers are happy with their jobs, they make themselves available to students, they run creative and supportive classes, and they have a keen eye for helping students shape and deepen their creative work. I'd say that the vast majority of writing instructors take their work in the classroom very seriously, and they enjoy the give-and-take of interacting with students. Good teachers are often good writers. They learn from their teaching and they learn from their students.

That said, I place faculty as number four in our criteria because it is not a certain or measurable aspect. As I noted earlier, some professors are on sabbatical, others move from program to program, others are terrific writers but lousy teachers. A good faculty is steady, generous with its time, and productive as writers.

Much about faculty, at least in this early stage of your selection process, is the luck of the draw. Perhaps one of your main professors will be on sabbatical for your first year. And perhaps that professor will be replaced with a visiting writer who understands and encourages your work. Perhaps this substitute is just what you need for your writing.

My point? The faculty criteria is unpredictable. That said, take a look at the faculty of your potential programs. Are there writers here whom you admire? Are there writers whom you might admire if you knew their work? Well, find their work in bookstores, in libraries, or online. Read it. Is there someone whom you admire in particular, someone who writes similar to you, or similar to how you'd like to write? Great. By all means, move this program up in your rankings. But keep in mind, someone who writes very differently from you may actually be a great help to you. You'll change as a writer as you move through a program. Keep faculty in mind, but keep it in perspective.

Don't you want to say something here about low-residency programs?

Yes. Faculty is going to matter much more in low-residency programs for three obvious reasons. First, location is not a priority since your location is where you're currently living. Second, funding is not a priority since low-residency programs offer few fellowships and scholarships. Third, your experience will be primarily with faculty, not with other students. Definitely narrow your choices, and then definitely read the work of the faculty on your list.

What about program size?

It's possible that this might be a big priority for you. Some programs admit as few as a ten students, others admit fifty or more. Three thoughts come to my mind:

1. Programs that accept a large number of students are more likely to include *you* in that large number of students. In other words, if one program accepts thirty students, and another only twelve, then just based on the law of averages you're more likely to be accepted to the larger program. As you narrow your list it may be wise to have a mix of smaller and larger programs.
2. Keep in mind that your experience in a creative writing program will rely in large part on your interactions with other graduate student writers. A larger program will feature more like-minded students and more not-like-minded students. Smaller programs, fewer for each. Do you like smaller groups or larger ones?
3. Finally, generally speaking, smaller programs are better in the funding aspect. They have fewer students to fund, and so they push their resources to these students.

Can you list the remaining criteria in bullet-point form?
Whatever seems best to you. I'm here to please.

- Perhaps you'd like to study in *more* than one genre (fiction, poetry, non-fiction, screenwriting, playwriting, children's fiction, etc.) Some schools offer this option, but most don't. If you're interested in this option, adjust your rankings accordingly.
- Two years or more? Most MFA programs are two years, though many are three years. Many of the MA programs will be one year, and, of course, PhD programs will be five years or more. The only thing I have to say about this is that I got most of my best writing done in the third year of my experience at the University of Massachusetts. How important is time to you? Do you have one or two years to devote to your craft, or do you have more? Adjust your rankings accordingly.
- Finally, do remember the other aspects of writing programs. Things like reading series, community outreach, and literary journals. It's my opinion that these aspects may be more important to you in the final selection process, and not as critical in this preliminary narrowing process. Sift your programs down to a dozen. Then apply. Then include these smaller, though important, criteria in your final selection process.

Chapter summary, please.
As you wish.

Chapter Summary

1. You can find a lot of preliminary information on creative writing program websites. I've listed them in the back of this book. A poorly designed website often indicates a poorly designed program. Information about funding, faculty, and other criteria should be directly stated and easy to find.

2. Location should be your first criteria in selecting a program. Make sure you'll live in a place where you'll be comfortable and challenged. Aspects like big city versus small college town, region of the country, and cultural amenities are important factors in making your program experience a success.

3. Funding should be your second criteria. And it's a close second. Unless you're independently wealthy, of course—then you've got lots of options. Seek programs that fund all or the majority of their graduate students. Avoid poorly funded programs. Keep in mind that programs that "tier" their students can sometimes create a competitive atmosphere. Information about funding should be clearly stated on the program website.

4. Teaching assistantships and fellowships are terrific ways to gain experience and improve your writing. They also provide funding, as do research and editorial assistantships. Avoid programs that offer *too much experience* (i.e., programs that require you to teach two or three classes a semester). A good program offers a good balance of experience and writing time.

5. The criteria in this chapter are for narrowing your schools and applying to those schools, not for making your final selection of where you want to attend. More on that in chapter 5.

6. A good faculty can make an enormously positive impact on your graduate experience. Possibly the most important impact. However, it's difficult to determine the level of teaching and availability of professors at this early stage. Leave that for your final selections. Do look at the faculty members of your prospective schools, and do read their work. However, location, funding, and teaching experience are much more important at this early stage.

7. Faculty is more important to low-residency programs at this early stage, as location and funding are likely already determined.

8. Program size is important for reasons of community, funding, and acceptance rate. Applying to a mix of smaller and larger programs might be a good idea.

9. Other factors to consider are flexibility in classes and genre, reading series, and literary journals.

Choosing a Low-Residency
MFA Program in Creative Writing

by Erika Dreifus

IN THE SIMPLEST TERMS, "low-residency" graduate programs (also called "brief-residency" programs) in creative writing offer the opportunity to study writing and earn an advanced degree without being based full-time on a university campus. Low-res students travel to campus intermittently (typically twice each year) for an intensive period (typically one to two weeks) of workshops, seminars, and readings. During the months between those sessions—or "residencies"—a low-res student writes (and reads) back at home, sending work to a faculty mentor and receiving feedback from that person. That remains the basic framework for most programs, with some variations we'll soon address.

A few years ago only a handful of these programs existed. The primary question a writer faced back then was: Should I apply to/attend a traditional or a low-residency program? The low-residency model is traceable to the mid-1970s, when poet Ellen Bryant Voigt established the first such program at Goddard College. A few years later, Voigt and others transferred their efforts and energies to a new location: Warren Wilson College. There simply weren't too many low-residency programs around to compete for attention. Or for students.

And the programs seemed fairly similar. Most focused on instruction in two or three primary genres; offered twice-yearly on-campus residencies with semesters during which students worked individually by correspondence with a faculty mentor; and required students to read extensively and write about literary craft issues with the same seriousness they devoted to generating and revising their own poetry or prose. They held particular appeal for those writers—including older adults—whose personal and/or professional commitments made the prospect of installing themselves on a university campus (quite possibly clear across the country) for two or more years of full-time graduate study more difficult than it might have been soon after finishing college however many years in the past.

That was then. Now there are more than thirty low-residency MFA programs. And even some of those students who may have the ability to relocate for a residential program are opting to go lo-res.

With the proliferation comes differentiation. And that means it's more important than ever to research programs and to understand the features and offerings that make each distinct. It's equally important for potential MFA students to think about their own writerly interests, needs, and goals, and to seek a felicitous match.

So how can you begin to distinguish among today's low-residency programs? What questions should you ask as you explore websites, or when you speak with program advisers, faculty, current students, or alumni? Here are eight topics that I recommend potential low-res students consider as they begin to assess the ever-increasing options.

1. Geography
You may think that geography shouldn't matter much when we're talking about low-residency programs. Think again.

First, you may need to factor transportation costs into your budget. For instance, the lowest roundtrip ticket for the Boston-Charlotte U.S. Airways route—the route I flew for each of my five MFA residencies at Queens University of Charlotte—currently costs $368 ("plus taxes and fees"). Multiply that by five (assuming costs remain stable over the next two years) and that's about another $2,000 to add to the MFA price tag. Plus lodging, meals, and ground transportation (not every location has good public transit).

Then, too, some people may consider enrolling in a low-residency program an opportunity to get to know (or revisit) a particular area. That was part of my reasoning when I chose the Queens program, based in the South, a part of the country I didn't know well at all. But others may simply prefer (or need) to stay closer to home.

And given the growth of these programs, it's now more likely that you can stay closer to home. Today there's a low-res program at Lesley University, based literally down the block away from my old apartment in Massachusetts. There's another at Pine Manor College just a few miles away. I can't imagine living in the Boston area and not giving those programs, and others in New England that were established after my application era, serious attention.

Similarly, writers living in or drawn to the Pacific Northwest will also find opportunities that simply did not exist back when I submitted applications in 2001. These options include programs based at Goddard College's Port Townsend, Washington, residency site; Pacific University; Pacific Lutheran University/Rainier Writing Workshop; Seattle Pacific University (its winter residency takes place on Whidbey Island, Washington; its summer residency is held at the Glen Workshop in Santa Fe, New Mexico); University of Alaska–Anchorage; University of British Columbia; and the Whidbey Writers Workshop.

Now that several public universities offer low-residency programs, geography matters in another, important respect: Tuition rates may differ markedly for in-state and out-of-state students. See, for a few examples, the programs offered by the University of Nebraska, Murray State University, the University of Alaska–Anchorage, and Eastern Kentucky University.

The Nebraska program's website, for instance, indicates per-semester tuition fees for Nebraskans of $2,895, more than reasonable when compared with other low-residency programs and especially appealing when contrasted with what Nebraska charges nonresidents: $7,346. At Murray State, residents from nearby counties in Tennessee, Illinois, and Indiana qualify for the same in-state tuition rates that apply to Kentucky residents, while writers living throughout Missouri, Tennessee, Illinois, and Indiana also receive a substantial discount from what is charged other out-of-state residents.

OK. Let's move on.

2. Genre

It may seem self-evident, but to some extent your low-residency options depend on your genre, and that's simply because not every low-residency program offers instruction in every genre. If you're only interested in writing for children/young adults, for instance, you'll have a more limited set of options than if you see yourself writing fiction or poetry for adults.

Some programs dedicate themselves exclusively to writing in a single genre, and you may find yourself drawn to that approach.

The Goucher College program in creative nonfiction, Hamline University's program in writing for children/young adults, and New England College's poetry program are three examples of such programs. On the other hand, you may find enriching and stimulating the presence and concomitant efforts and contributions of faculty and fellow students working in other genres, as well as programwide readings and seminars in those areas outside your own concentration.

You may also want to investigate specific opportunities to study or specialize in more than one genre. At the University of British Columbia's optional residency program, for instance, students are required to work in at least three genres (seven are offered: fiction, poetry, nonfiction, writing for children, translation, stage play, and screenwriting).

3. Faculty

What a program may teach you—how to write fiction, poetry, nonfiction, and/or another genre—is one important consideration. Another is who will be doing the teaching.

Learn about a program's faculty members. What have they published? Where have they taught? How long have they taught? Not every great writer is a great teacher (and vice versa).

Moreover, not every great classroom teacher is a great mentor from a distance or online workshop facilitator. How much experience does the faculty have with teaching in the particular low-residency format? How accessible can you expect them to be?

Some programs and program websites make it easier for you to learn about faculty than others. But even without a program's help you can do some relatively simple detective work. At the very least, a program website will include a list of faculty names. Armed with that, you can begin some easy Internet research.

Many faculty maintain their own author websites and/or blogs. Check these out. Read stories, essays, poems, reviews (not just reviews of their work, but reviews they've written of others'), and/or excerpts they may have linked to. If a faculty author will be appearing in your area, try to attend the event.

Many faculty are full-time professors, often at universities other than the one where the low-residency program is based. If that's the case, you can probably discover something about their courses and teaching interests at their primary institution's website.

It's important to remember that faculty lives and plans are subject to the same variations as those of their students. So it's a good idea not to base your application or enrollment plans on the presence of any one or two names on a program's faculty listing. Someone whose name appears there when you apply may be on leave when you enroll, or may leave before you've graduated.

4 and 5. Program Requirements and Program Structure
These are multifaceted and overlapping issues. What they boil down to is this: How will your learning unfold?

You'll likely want to know about reading lists and assignments. How are these devised? How much reading should you expect? Some writers are wary of what's often termed a "critical" paper that many programs require in addition to the creative thesis. But in most cases, the "critical" paper is less a work of literary theory than research into and analysis of craft issues, and it can be an important (not to mention publishable) part of low-residency studies.

You'll also want to know more about the residencies. When/how often do they take place and where? We've already mentioned that Seattle Pacific University's program holds residencies in two locations. Similarly, Carlow University's program is based in Pittsburgh, Pennsylvania, but its residencies alternate between the home campus and Ireland. There are other examples. On the other hand, residencies are indeed "optional" for students in the University of British Columbia's "optional residency" program (I'm told that the vast majority of students do opt to participate in the once-yearly residencies).

Be sure you understand the program's workshop policy. Most programs will have you "workshop" your manuscript(s) in a group while on campus, receiving critiques on your writing from fellow students and from an instructor at the residencies while sending work (via mail or e-mail) only to your assigned faculty mentor at predetermined points between residencies. The one-to-one work with a faculty member that focuses on your own submissions to that person is the basis for what's sometimes called "the mentor-and-packet" model of low-residency instruction. One of its touted advantages is the close attention the work receives from an expert source, similar to that from a truly dedicated editor.

But I've sometimes wondered what happens when a student-mentor pairing doesn't work. That's one of the reasons I opted for a program that maintains an online workshop structure during the semester (Queens University of Charlotte uses this instead of the individualized mentor approach.) With online workshops, students submit their work (and comments on each others' work) to each other and an instructor throughout the semester as well as during the residencies. (At Queens, I frankly found some student feedback more constructive than I found instructor comments.)

Which system do you prefer, and why? Ask how each functions. If a workshop system remains in place, what training do less work-shop-savvy students receive in critiques and how do faculty ensure and sustain quality feedback each semester? How exactly does the online system work, logistically? However the program goes about the essential work of teaching, how are your particular instructors/workshop leaders selected—how are those matches made? Do you have any say in the process?

Finally, what other requirements does the program have, and how do they complement your essential work on your poetry or prose? At Lesley University, for example, an "interdisciplinary com-ponent" requires students to pursue three semester-long projects outside their exchanges with their mentors. Some students take a course in a field that complements their writing (someone writing historical fiction might take a history class, for instance). Other projects have included independent studies in website design or children's book illustration, or a subject I myself have helped Lesley students pursue: book reviewing. And still others involve students in paid or nonpaid internships in editing, publishing, or teaching. Several other programs have similar requirements and offerings, sometimes called "enrichment projects" or "practica." Some poten-tial MFA students worry that these requirements may detract from their focus on their primary work. Others view them as nourish-ing that work and providing practical experience that will be useful in their professional careers beyond the MFA. Again, you need to have a good sense of your own needs, goals, and interests.

6. Special Offerings
Remember what I said before about differentiation? The blossom-ing of MFA programs has, perhaps inevitably, begun to lead to some very specific approaches. Seattle Pacific University's program, for example, describes itself as a program for those "who not only want to pursue excellence in the craft of writing but also place their

work within the larger context of the Judeo-Christian tradition of faith." The fully online (technically, a "no-residency") program at the University of Texas–El Paso can be completed entirely in English, entirely in Spanish, or bilingually. Chatham University's low-residency program describes itself as sharing the focus for which Chatham's traditional residential program is recognized: nature, environment, and travel writing.

You may be attracted to a program that has its own literary journal or press. You may be drawn to the option of spending at least one residency abroad. A good program will publicize its special features on its website. Again, it's up to you to evaluate those offerings in light of your own preferences and goals.

7. Student and Alumni Achievement/Employment

It isn't necessarily fair to compare the records of new programs with ones that have been around for decades, but it is absolutely fair to ask how programs and their faculty help students transition into careers as professional writers. Relevant questions might include, "What happens when a faculty member thinks a given story/poem/essay is publishable?" or "What counseling is offered students for post-MFA publication and job options?" Although some people may insist on the MFA's purely "artistic" purpose, many others approach it as a professional degree. Ostensibly you're receiving some real training for the time, money, and effort you're devoting here. If that matters to you, make sure it matters to the program, too.

8. Financial Aid

The full-tuition awards many traditional programs confer on their MFA students are exceedingly rare, although not altogether absent, in the low-residency world. Moreover, many of the paying teaching fellowships/assistantships awarded by traditional programs rely on the MFA students' presence on campus to teach undergraduate composition and creative writing classes. If you're crossing the continent for a residency, that work's not feasible.

To a considerable degree, one of the early principles of low-residency study holds fast today: by allowing you to remain in your pre-MFA place of residence, a low-residency program also presumably allows you to remain in your pre-MFA job and keep that paycheck coming to help you meet your MFA expenses. Therefore, many low-residency programs offer only a limited number of small grants and scholarships. Loans, unfortunately, tend to be the primary source to help finance low-residency MFA study.

What this means is that you shouldn't rely on the low-res program itself to help you pay for your studies. Look beyond it. Your research may uncover some less obvious sources for grants, scholarships, and low- or no-interest loans. Places to begin your research online include the graduate scholarships, fellowships, and loans information maintained by Jon Harrison at the Michigan State University Libraries (http://lib.msu.edu/harris23/grants/3/gradinf. htm), and the UCLA Graduate and Postdoctoral External Support (GRAPES) Database (http://www.gdnet.ucla.edu/grpinst.htm).

As with everything else, however, be sure to check with any program that interests you for the latest information. Sometimes there are happy developments, as occurred in 2007, when the Whidbey Writers Workshop program announced a new full-tuition merit scholarship.

Finally, there are the intangibles. How difficult (or easy) is it to receive answers to your questions? Does the program seem eager to help by posting comprehensive and up-to-date information on its website, or by responding promptly and professionally via phone or e-mail?

Choosing a low-residency MFA program these days is—or should be—a highly individualized process. The more thought you devote to the enterprise the more likely it is that you'll make a good "match" for yourself, and for your writing.

ADDITIONAL RESOURCES

- At Erika Dreifus's Practicing Writing Blog (http://practicing-writing.blogspot.com):
  - list of links to low-residency and summer study graduate programs in creative writing (http://practicing-writing.blogspot.com/2007/08/low-residency-or-summer-study-mfa-and_28.html)
  - low-residency MFA funding info (http://practicing-writing.blogspot.com/2005/11/on-subject-of-funding-for-low.html)

- "The Scoop on Low-Residency MFA Programs." *First Draft*, Fall 2004, 34–37. This article, based largely on the author's experience in Spalding University's program, is also available for download online: http://www.writersforum.org/firstdraft.
- Poets & Writers Speakeasy discussion board. Multiple threads address low-residency programs. http://www.pw.org/speakeasy.

Is the PhD in Creative Writing the MFA of the Future?

by Ed Schwarzschild

So, YOU'RE THINKING ABOUT AN MFA, or you're working on an MFA, or you're already the proud recipient of an MFA. No matter where you are on your path, you're holding this book in your hands and now would be an excellent time to consider a PhD in creative writing. Though the PhD option has been mentioned in these pages, it's possible to have reached this point in the book without a full sense of the specific benefits and requirements of such programs. Allow me, then, to continue more or less where the esteemed Adam Johnson left off.

First, a few necessary disclosures and a little personal background: I don't have a PhD in Creative Writing. I do have a PhD in English (Washington U in St. Louis), an MA in Creative Writing (Boston U), and I was a Stegner Fellow. For the last seven years, I've been teaching fiction workshops and contemporary literature at the University at Albany, SUNY, where we have a strong, innovative PhD in creative writing program (I am, of course, biased, but you can judge our program for yourself). Though the traditional PhD path worked well for me, I wish I had known more about the PhD in creative writing when I was thinking about graduate school. I wish I had known more about many things, actually. In any case, add me to the chorus: where was *this* book when I needed it? Back in 1986, when I was a senior undergrad, the little I heard about PhDs in creative writing was dismissive, mostly because those programs were rare and relatively unknown entities. Also, their job placement records were unclear. If you wanted a career as a writer and a professor, the traditional PhD seemed to be by far your surest bet.

For me, at that point, the clincher between the MFA and the PhD was the time I would be given to read. I'd been premed all through my undergrad years (as the oldest child of parents who didn't get to go to college I was, of course, supposed to become a fabulously wealthy brain surgeon), but I fell in love with fiction writing during my freshman year. Denied it through a few years of chemistry, bio, calculus, and physics, but after I registered for the MCAT the third time and *still* couldn't bring myself to take the damn test, I read the writing on the wall, so to speak, and took the GRE, including the subject exam in literature. If it hadn't been clear before, that literature exam made it painfully obvious that I needed to read more. A lot more.

And St. Louis turned out to be a wonderful place to read and write. Apartments were spacious and cheap, I met a handful of kindred spirits, and we inspired each other, talking books constantly, reading each others work, and dining for free at the city's plentiful and bountiful happy hours. Still, though the PhD was supposedly the surest path to gainful academic employment, many of us had our doubts, and we all knew several people who had finished their degrees and remained unemployed. I remember talking about this problem with one of the department's most senior professors—a great teacher named Naomi Lebowitz, famous for her impassioned discussions about everyone from Balzac to Ibsen to Svevo; famous, too, for her ever-present dachsund, Miss Marple. As usual, she had memorable lines to share. She acknowledged that there was some truth to the rumors we'd heard about the way the old old boys' network used to be: in those bygone days, you finished your PhD and then your adviser made a phone call and then you had a job and your career went on from there. "I can't guarantee a job to anyone," Lebowitz said. "All I can promise you is the chance to read and write and study for at least five years in a good, solid community of fellow writers and readers. And, trust me, that means more than you might think."

I didn't catch the wisdom right away—I *wanted* her to guarantee me a job!—but I got it eventually, and I've repeated it to my students over the years. And it remains the essential, undeniable benefit of pursuing a PhD—of any kind. The gift of extended time and space to pursue your passion cannot be overestimated.

But there are some requirements about how you spend that extended time in these programs. I'll explain the basic structure of

the PhD in creative writing, using the Albany program as a repre-
sentative example. The fundamental elements of our program are:

1. Course Work
2. The Foreign Language Requirement
3. The Qualifying Examination
4. The Dissertation
5. Teaching

And here are more details:

1. Course Work
You need to accumulate seventy-two credits and this will typically
take anywhere from three to six semesters, depending on how many
credits you bring with you. You can bring in as many as thirty and
people who have already complete MAs or MFAs tend to do exactly
that. The courses you'll take will include a mix of workshop/craft
classes and literature/theory classes. Different programs have different kinds of distribution requirements. Most of them used to be
based on chronologically arranged periods and a handful of "major"
authors. For better or worse (a subject of much debate; Google
"canon wars"), the requirements have become much more flexible.
The program at Albany is no exception. We now have four very
broad concentrations, ranging from "Literature, Modernity, and the
Contemporary" to "Writing Practices." Students are required both
to select a primary concentration (at least sixteen credits) and to
take courses outside of their chosen concentration (at least eight
credits). Though there are only four required courses, the structure
encourages students to develop depth and breadth. It no longer
insures that every student will have read Milton and Chaucer.

2. The Foreign Language Requirement
This is simple and can be satisfied two ways, via demonstrated
"reading level" in two languages (based on exams or course work) or
"fluency" in one language (based on exams or course work).

3. The Qualifying Examination
This marks the transition from course work to writing the dissertation. These exams require you, in consultation with your adviser
and others, to compose reading lists and rationales for the lists in

advance. You then have to pass a written and oral exam based on the lists and the rationales. The entire examination process is designed to prepare each student to be ready to write the dissertation he or she want to write.

4. The Dissertation
Here's the language straight from our webpage: "Students are allowed considerable latitude with regard to the dissertation's form and focus. Dissertations may take such forms as critical argument, fiction, poetry, reports of empirical research, or drama; they may also feature some mixture of these. . . . The dissertation will ordinarily grow out of the student's course work and even more directly out of the qualifying examination, and is designed so that the student can complete it within the academic year following the examination."

5. Teaching
After the first year of course work, PhD students typically teach one course each semester. When considering a PhD program, teaching (courses and course load) and funding are two of the most important factors to keep in mind, for reasons this handbook has already made clear.

When the requirements of the program are listed in this way, I think it's easy to see how each of these discrete tasks can improve and inspire one's writing while also offering perfect preparation for working in an actual, living, breathing English department.

But there are still a few important, frequently asked questions.

Question 1: Will my writing get lost amid the various requirements?
The requirements will inspire and instruct, but they will also at times slow your writing. This is undeniable. But ask yourself if the requirements and demands of the PhD program interfere with your writing more than any "normal" job or whatever else you might be doing instead of the PhD program?

Question 2: Will I be forced to read and understand inscrutable critical theory?
You will, in almost every program, at some time or another, be required to read and comment upon critical theory and some of it

may be difficult to understand. But that isn't necessarily a bad thing, for at least two reasons: (1) you might actually enjoy some of it; (2) you'll be able to talk more easily with your colleagues, current and future, and they, in turn will be able to talk more easily with you.

Consider it, in cases of extreme resistance, as the equivalent of an extra foreign language requirement: it's useful learning, something that will help you to be a better citizen of the world, and if not the world, then certainly your department.

Because, okay, let's finally face it straight up, like the MFA, the PhD is at the end of the day a credential. It is a credential that qualifies you for a teaching position. Once you get the teaching position, you'll be working in an English department somewhere. Some of your colleagues will be writers of fiction, nonfiction, poetry, and drama. But many of them will be theorists and Shakespeareans, American studies scholars, eighteenth-century specialists, medievalists, and so on. The PhD in creative writing not only gives you more time and space to work on your first book or two, but it also prepares you to work in an English department—to converse with your colleagues and your students—in a way that an MFA simply cannot. Hiring committees understand this. Of course, as always, your published books trump everything, but given the choice between two roughly equal candidates, one with an MFA and one with a PhD, I think the PhD would almost always win out. This only becomes more true as universities and colleges confront financial challenges.

I hate to mention that market-oriented aspect of it, but there it is. I, of course, did it all ass-backwards: got the PhD, then a teaching job, then went back for an MA in Creative Writing and the Stegner, and then got another teaching job. So, you can do it that way, too. I like to think that I was just practicing what I would one day preach. I mean, it's true, I believe English departments would be better places if all the people with creative writing degrees had PhDs. But I also believe that English departments would be much better places if all the people with traditional PhDs went back to get creative writing degrees. What a world that would be!

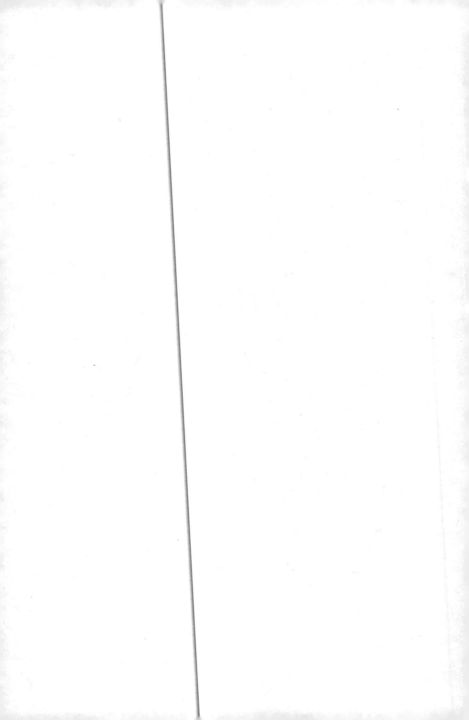

CHAPTER 3

The Programs

by Seth Abramson

Note from Tom Kealey:

Over the past three years Seth Abramson has provided an amazing ser-vice to potential MFAers on his website The Suburban Ecstasies (http://sethabramson.blogspot.com). You'll find information there about MFA acceptance rates, graduate awards, graduate placement, program rank-ings, and application response times. It's really an incredible site, and to say that I've been blown away by the work that Seth has put into it would be an understatement. When I sat down to rewrite chapter 3 for this updated MFA Handbook, my first thought was, "This is silly. Seth knows this better than I do." And he does. So, I'm stepping aside, and I'm very grateful for all of the work he's put into this chapter. I think readers will be, too.

Two things readers should know: Seth Abramson attends the Iowa Writers Workshop, and I attended the University of Massachusetts and the Stegner Fellowships.

Thanks Seth!

First Ranking

Assessing MFA program quality is such a difficult task that the first major news outlet ever to attempt it, *U.S. News & World Report*, gave up almost immediately—back in 1997. The prevailing wis-dom then, as now, was that unlike every other type of graduate program in America, the MFA is singularly ineligible for any sort of ranking, and cannot be analyzed, to any extent, using hard data. I disagree, and have always disagreed, and for that reason began in late 2006 to create (or attempt to create) new approaches for the assessment of MFA programs.

The first thing I found was that the institutional factors that *U.S. News* determined couldn't be measured for MFA programs actually *can't* be measured—not just for MFA programs, but for any type of educational program. As I continued my research, then, it became clear that the only logical reason for *U.S. News* ceasing to rank creative writing programs in 1997 would have been that the programs themselves had either not released the necessary hard data to the magazine or else had never been asked to do so. This was the only logical reason, because all of the measures available to *U.S. News* for ranking every *other* type of educational program were, in fact, available for MFA programs. Indeed, as I embarked on this long journey toward the creation of new MFA rankings I found myself puzzled trying to figure out why acceptance rates can be calculated for undergraduate programs but not for MFA programs. Or, for instance, why it's impossible to calculate the financial resources of an MFA program based upon its financial aid offerings. Class sizes, student-to-faculty ratios, program durations— all of these factors were obviously amenable to comparison and cataloging, so why had *U.S. News* dropped the ball? I'm not sure that, even now, there's a definitive answer to that question, except to say that it's obvious the ball *was* dropped, and that it was inevitable that, at some point in the future, someone would eventually pick it up. The rankings and analyses that follow are an attempt to carry on the task that *U.S. News* inexplicably abandoned more than a decade ago.

One of the fundamental premises behind these rankings and analyses is that they ought not be the primary determinants behind where any applicant chooses to apply. The most important factors behind an application to an MFA program will *always* be personal, and therefore impossible to catalog. That said, it's important to remember, too, that many of the assessments we conclude are "our own" are every bit as subjective as the sort of points-based, reputation-only ranking system *U.S. News* developed and then discarded back in the 1990s. For instance, can you learn anything about a program by attending one of its workshops? No, because every professor runs his or her workshop differently, and no two are alike. How about a campus visit? Can that establish, in the mind of a prospective applicant, a genuine sense of how it would be to attend that program? Again, no, as during a campus visit the program being visited is manifestly attempting to sell you on its allure, and cannot—and likely does not—present to the applicant an unbiased picture of what life in that program would be like. What about talking to current students? Surely *that* is advised, right? And indeed, it most certainly is; at the same time, unless an applicant speaks to more than a handful of current students at any given MFA program, there's a real danger of getting only an incomplete picture of that school's offerings. Any student currently in an MFA program will tell you that for every student there who'd say one thing about their program, there are two others who would say another thing entirely. The honest answer to any query about the quality of a program is this: It depends on who you talk to. And so the question becomes whether or not prospective applicants are willing to risk the next two or three years of their lives, and possibly tens of thousands of dollars, on the possibility of having caught an MFA student on a particularly bad day (say, immediately after she or he has had an unusually bruising workshop session). It seems clear that so-called hard data must be *some* part of the application decision—even if, as is clear, it absolutely cannot and must not constitute the greater part of it. Location, for instance, can never be assessed mathematically (except as to cost-of-living indicators). But of course, this same maxim—that location is a vital, yet unquantifiable piece in the average applicant's matriculation decision—holds true for *every* ranking of educational institutions *U.S. News & World Report* has ever done. MFA programs, as it turns out, are simply not as different as we'd been led to believe.

Perhaps it's no surprise, then, that the number of factors amenable to hard-data analysis, in terms of the quality of any one MFA program, is considerable. These factors include the following: size of entering class (and further broken down by individual genre); acceptance rate; student-to-faculty ratio; individual workshop size; dollar value of average financial aid package; duration of program; type of degree awarded (MA or MFA); age of program; number of visiting faculty per year; ratio of faculty members in one genre as compared to another; major prizes won by faculty and recent graduates; percentage of faculty at top programs who themselves attended one institution or another; and many, many more. Several of the above measures are employed by *U.S. News* to distinguish among various undergraduate programs, law schools, medical schools, business schools, engineering schools, and nearly every other type of graduate or undergraduate educational program. Perhaps, then, it is not that MFA programs were considered by *U.S. News* to be different than these other programs, but instead merely not worth the trouble—as who's less interested in "hard data" than artists (or so the thinking may have gone)? What I've found in the past couple of years, however, is that, as one of the fastest-growing fields of graduate study in the United States, creative writing absolutely *is* typified by applicants who desire to know, just as much as their peers planning legal and medical careers, which program will be the right fit for them. And hard data is most certainly a part of that picture.

The first of the rankings included below isn't really a ranking at all; it's a poll. This nonscientific study was conducted across a fourteen-month period at the Speakeasy, the online discussion board run by *Poets & Writers* magazine. The respondents were registered users of the Speakeasy, and were differentiated by their individual user accounts. Essentially, the methodology for the poll was this: users' lists of programs—either programs a user was intending to apply to, or else programs a user considered to be the best in America—were tallied within a single data-source, with each mention of a school constituting one "vote." The result of that compilation is the poll below. While, as noted, the poll is unscientific, it nevertheless represents the largest poll of MFA applicants (scientific or otherwise) ever done. Moreover, while it's impossible to calculate the statistical "confidence" level of the poll, it should be noted that the individual data sets compiled during the 2006–7 and 2007–8 application cycles suggest consistency in programs' placement over time. While genre-specific polls were also taken during the 2007–8 application cycle, in addition to the all-genre poll, thus far the number of respondents for these polls is too small to be statistically or even informally significant. It is important to note also that while the *Poets & Writers* website was the data-collection point for what is termed below the "P&W Reader Poll Top 100," neither *Poets & Writers* nor any of their agents or affiliates in any way sponsored or endorsed this poll, and the term "P&W" is used here merely to denote the forum within which the relevant data was collected.

Explanations for, and discussions of, the second and third rankings listed in this chapter precede those individual rankings.

P&W Reader Poll Top 100

(with votes in parentheses; t = tie)

1.   University of Iowa (115)
2.   University of Michigan (81)
3.   University of Massachusetts (80)
4t. University of Texas (71)
4t. University of Virginia (71)
6.   Cornell University (66)
7.   Indiana University (64)
8t. Brown University (57)
8t. Syracuse University (57)
10. University of California at Irvine (48)
11. University of Oregon (47)
12. University of Montana (44)
13t. University of Notre Dame (40)
13t. University of Washington (40)
15. Johns Hopkins University (38)
16. Columbia University (37)
17. University of Minnesota (34)
18. New York University (32)
19. University of Wisconsin (31)
20. University of North Carolina at Wilmington (30)
21. University of Houston (29)
22t. University of Arizona (26)
22t. Washington University at St. Louis (26)
24. The New School (25)
25. Ohio State University (23)
26t. Sarah Lawrence College (22)
26t. University of North Carolina at Greensboro (22)
28t. Hollins University (21)
28t. University of Alabama (21)
28t. University of Florida (21)
31t. George Mason University (20)
31t. Purdue University (20)

31t. University of Arkansas (20)
31t. University of Illinois (20)
35. Florida State University (19)
36t. Arizona State University (18)
36t. Colorado State University (18)
38t. University of New Hampshire (17)
38t. University of Pittsburgh (17)
40. Brooklyn College (16)
41t. Boston University (15)
41t. Bowling Green State University (15)
43. University of California at Davis (13)
44t. Emerson College (12)
44t. San Francisco State University (12)
44t. Texas State University (12)
47. Hunter College [CUNY] (11)
48t. Pennsylvania State University (10)
48t. University of New Mexico (10)
50t. California School of the Arts [CalArts] (8)
50t. New Mexico State University (8)
50t. School of the Art Institute of Chicago (8)
50t. Southern Illinois University (8)
50t. University of Mississippi (8)
50t. Vanderbilt University (8)
56t. University of Colorado (6)
56t. University of San Francisco (6)
56t. Western Michigan University (6)
59t. American University (5)
59t. Rutgers University at Newark (5)
59t. Saint Mary's College [CA] (5)
59t. University of Nevada at Las Vegas (5)
63. San Diego State University (4)
64t. Eastern Washington University (3)
64t. Louisiana State University (3)
64t. University of British Columbia [Canada] (3)
64t. University of Maryland (3)
64t. University of Utah (3)
69t. Columbia College [IL] (2)
69t. Florida International University (2)
69t. Mills College (2)
69t. North Carolina State University (2)

69t. Northern Michigan University (2)
69t. San Jose State University (2)
69t. University of Baltimore (2)
69t. University of Idaho (2)
69t. University of Kansas (2)
69t. Virginia Commonwealth University (2)
79t. Boise State University (1)
79t. California College of the Arts [CCA] (1)
79t. Minnesota State University at Mankato (1)
79t. Minnesota State University at Moorhead (1)
79t. Old Dominion University (1)
79t. Oregon State University (1)
79t. Rutgers University at Camden (1)
79t. University of California at Riverside (1)
79t. University of Memphis (1)
79t. University of Miami (1)
79t. University of South Carolina (1)
79t. University of Texas at El Paso (1)
79t. University of Wyoming (1)
79t. West Virginia University (1)
79t. Wichita State University (1)

[N = 288].

Second Ranking
The importance of funding in assessing a program's attractiveness to prospective students cannot be overstated. In just the past ten years, those programs that seem to have made the greatest strides (reputation-wise) since the program rankings of the mid-1990s have been, almost without exception, colleges and universities of national reputation that added to their name-recognition value the additional value of an excellent financial aid package. The rise of programs at the University of Texas, University of Notre Dame, University of Minnesota, University of Wisconsin, and, more recently, Ohio State University, Purdue University, and Vanderbilt University, can be seen as a sign of things to come. When nationally recognized educational institutions decide to unveil top-notch funding packages, prospective students pay attention, and application numbers rise, even when those programs are new and as yet untested. The

reason for this, of course, is the one piece of conventional wisdom almost all MFA applicants subscribe to: as the MFA is not a professional degree, and does not guarantee employment in any professional field, it is not a degree for which a student should go into significant debt. The MFA is an "art school" degree, which in no way devalues its many attractions but certainly puts into perspective the sort of financial considerations one should have in mind when deciding to apply. Indeed, it would seem that, in just the past five years, funding has surpassed faculty and reputation to become the second-most important consideration for applicants (with the most important factor continuing to be, for most prospective MFA students, location). As conceded at the beginning of this chapter, the notion of "location" is not amenable to ranking, and so it would seem that a funding ranking is the next best thing.

The creation of this first-ever funding-only ranking of creative writing programs was predicated on several presumptions: first, that programs will advertise their funding packages to their best effect on their individual websites; second, that it should not be incumbent upon students to have to hunt down, through phone calls and e-mails, data on funding; third, that many programs presently do little enough to articulate their specific funding packages to prospective students that, until the programs on their own initiative decide to provide this information publicly and in detail, any ranking system will be at best an approximation.

All of the above taken into account, what follows is likely the most comprehensive and researched funding-based ranking done to date—simply because it's the *only* one. While it is true that to the extent some programs may have inadvertently misreported or underreported their aid packages on their websites those programs may be at an advantage or disadvantage in this ranking, the expectation is that each time this ranking is researched and presented it will become more and more an accurate reflection of the current state of affairs at each program. Certainly, this ranking's reliance on promotional materials assumes—as it seems only reasonable to assume—that these promotional materials, put out by the colleges and universities themselves, are accurate and as detailed as the programs intend and want them to be.

In creating the rankings below, numerous factors were taken into account for each program, including the following: the relative cost of living in the town or city where the program is located;

the number of teaching, research, journal-based, and administrative assistantships, or funded internships, available per entering class; the percentage of tuition remission attached to each assistantship; the stipend associated with each assistantship; the availability of health care coverage as part of any stipend, and/or coverage of other miscellaneous student fees; the number of fellowships and scholarships available to incoming students; whether these fellowships and scholarships are need-based, merit-based, or both (with a preference, as this is primarily a ranking for those concerned about their finances, for need-based fellowships); assignment of limited or full tuition remission to fellowships and scholarships; the number of years for which funding is guaranteed, to the extent it is guaranteed; the renewability of assistantships; the frequency with which students must apply for financial aid review; uniformity of financial aid packages (with uniformity seen as a generally positive thing, because it suggests locked-in funding for all students); availability of in-state and out-of-state tuition waivers, or grants, for students without assistantships; availability of discretionary funds for study abroad, student travel, or miscellaneous student expenses; and the availability of postgraduate fellowships, grants, and scholarships through the program. In rare instances, such as to break ties between schools, consideration was given to the size of the program, as experience shows that it is easier for a small program to initiate creative schemes to fund students who would otherwise be underfunded than it is for a large program to address a funding shortfall for a larger number of program admittees.

One of the benefits of creating this ranking, as can be seen from the above, is giving prospective MFA students a sense of those factors by which they can distinguish between aid packages at different schools. To the extent students choose to contact programs to which they've been admitted to get more information about financial aid awards, these are the sorts of considerations they should keep in mind and the types of issues they should inquire about with program representatives.

It should be noted, too, that financial aid packages were assessed, for this ranking, on a "percentage-of-class" basis rather than on an "absolute-number" basis. Were this ranking intended primarily for the benefit of the programs themselves—as a way for them to compare their financial resources with those of other programs—going about things this way would be counterintuitive, as it would effectively reward small programs for being small, while punishing programs that (due to their size) almost certainly offer more full-aid packages than their smaller peers, numerically speaking, but are able to offer such packages to only a small (or simply smaller) percentage of their incoming class. Because this ranking is intended for students, however—more particularly, for the "average" student admitted to any of the programs below—it is concerned with *percentages* moreso than absolute numbers. The "average" student, the one situated right in the middle of any bell curve of successful applicants to a given program, doesn't care (nor need he or she care) how many full-aid packages a program offers. All things being equal, the average student merely wishes to know the likelihood that he or she will receive such a package. And because this ranking aims to help answer that question, percentages, and not absolute numbers, are the focus here. Applicants should therefore view this ranking as answering the fundamental question, "If I'm admitted to this school, what are my chances of getting good funding?"

The first thing that becomes clear when one attempts a large-scale assessment of MFA funding packages is that there is, in fact, a sort of consistent "code" programs use to describe their offerings—and probably will continue to be, until programs begin opting for total transparency as a rule of thumb. For instance, as to the availability of assistantships, the nearly three hundred MFA programs in the United States seemed to break down their financial aid schemes using the following terminology: "full-class availability," "virtually full-class availability," "most [students]," "the majority," "many," "[awarded] on a competitive basis," "[awarded] on a very competitive basis," "limited availability," "very limited availability," and "single-student availability." In several instances—though this was rare—programs advertised a specific number of available assistantships, which number could then be translated into the hierarchy above, depending upon the overall size of the program (obviously, "two to six" assistantships means one thing in a program of ten incoming students, and quite another when the entering class is more than sixty strong). While using the above terminology to compare assistantship availability is an inexact science at best, it is also quite evidently the best system any prospective student can hope to employ under the current regime of financial aid package reporting. Indeed, it would surprise many prospective applicants to learn that only a minority of programs are willing to reveal their assistantship stipends in promotional materials—even though, by and large, these numbers are at least generally known to the programs at all times.

It seems odd that one of the most grave and abiding concerns of prospective applicants is treated in such an uneven fashion by the nation's MFA programs, and the lack of trustworthy available information was certainly a significant impetus behind the creation of this ranking. While imperfect, the Abramson/Kealey Funding Ranking is a start, and a comprehensive and well-researched one at that. Still, it will require a significant effort on the part of the programs themselves to fully answer the questions about funding—nearly all of which have been itemized in this brief introduction—that almost every single MFA applicant nationwide is confronted with each fall.

Generally speaking, if a program is *not* listed here—either in the ranking proper or in the Honorable Mention section—prospective students should assume that, if admitted, they would *more likely than not* find that significant funding is unavailable to them. In other words, while this ranking may be merely a curiosity for applicants for whom funding is not an issue, all things being equal, applicants with even *moderate* financial need will find this ranking an important and perhaps even vital resource, both for ruling programs in and ruling programs out. As a general principle, and as indicated throughout this *Handbook*, poets and writers should *not* go into substantial debt for an MFA degree. If the MFA degree were, strictly speaking, a "professional" degree—that is, one that *in itself* immediately qualified a graduate for a specific form of professional employment—that would be one thing; but it isn't, and so the rule of thumb outlined in this *Handbook* seems a sound one.

Abramson/Kealey Funding Ranking

1. University of Texas
2. University of Michigan
3. Cornell University
4. University of Florida
5t. Indiana University
5t. Purdue University
5t. University of Wisconsin

8t.   University of Alabama
8t.   Vanderbilt University
10.   Louisiana State University
11t. University of Minnesota
11t. University of Oregon
11t. Ohio State University
11t. Syracuse University
11t. Arizona State University
16t. Johns Hopkins University
16t. Pennsylvania State University
18.   University of California at Irvine
19.   Brown University
20.   University of Virginia
21.   University of Houston
22.   Washington University at St. Louis
23t. University of Illinois
23t. McNeese State University
23t. University of Iowa
26.   University of Nevada at Las Vegas
27.   Southern Illinois University
28.   University of Arkansas
29.   Virginia Tech University
30.   Old Dominion University
31t. University of Notre Dame
31t. West Virginia University
33t. Florida State University
33t. Georgia College & State University
35.   Wichita State University
36.   Virginia Commonwealth University
37.   University of Idaho
38.   University of Montana
39.   University of North Carolina at Greensboro
40.   Minnesota State University at Mankato
41.   Colorado State University
42t. University of Massachusetts at Amherst
42t. University of Mississippi
44.   University of Miami
45.   University of Alaska at Fairbanks
46.   University of Wyoming
47.   University of North Carolina at Wilmington

48. University of New Orleans
49. Bowling Green State University
50t. George Mason University
50t. University of New Mexico

Honorable Mention (in alphabetical order): Boise State University; Boston University; Eastern Washington University; Rutgers University at Newark; San Diego State University; University of Arizona; University of California at Riverside; Northern Michigan University; University of Colorado; University of Kansas; University of New Hampshire; University of South Carolina; University of Washington.

Third Ranking

The only thing more controversial than creating a tiered ranking of creative writing programs is creating a nontiered numerical one. Still, with the creation of the first-ever large-scale poll of program popularity, and the first-ever funding-only ranking of programs, it seems only natural for these two measures to be roughly conjoined, along with the other significant factors referenced in this chapter, and for a broadly delineated overall ranking to emerge.

Needless to say, comprehensive tiered rankings are both limited and defined by the factors that can and cannot be taken into account. For instance, a decision was made here not to consider location, as whether applicants prefer heat or cold, the mountains or the beaches, east or west, north or south is entirely up to them, and cannot be quantified by anyone else. Likewise, determining how to factor in a program's size is a tricky business: some students want a better student-to-faculty ratio and more one-on-one access to faculty, and some students want to see as many different faces as possible in their workshops, and have the largest possible social environment in which to live and write.

In contrast to size, the quality of funding packages can be roughly agreed upon and quantified, as can—through polling—the enthusiasm with which students are presently treating individual programs. Acceptance rates and class sizes can be partially quantified—"partially" only because not all programs release this information, though in an ideal world all of them would. Placement data, which tracks the number of a program's graduates placed at the highest levels of the academy, and honors-based data, which tracks the various accolades won by program graduates, are only recently becoming available and again are only partial in nature.

Overall reputation, contrary to the claims of the mid-1990s MFA rankings, probably cannot be quantified, except for the few programs whose reputation in one or more genres is so well-established as to be essentially beyond dispute. Still, given that the surge in popularity of the creative writing MFA degree has largely occurred over the last ten to fifteen years, most programs are relatively new—and even "older" programs have not, by and large, been around for long enough to truly create a sort of "timelessness" to their prestige. Thus it becomes necessary to rely primarily on known data points for any analysis, and, where necessary (that is, only for the rare tie-breaker) on the "general sense impression" of the present authors, who've tried to spend enough time tracking programs to make their opinions worthy of the readership of this *Handbook*.

Without a doubt, one flaw in creating a tiered system is that there will often be significant discrepancies among the schools within a single tier. Some schools are likely to be seen as residing at the latter end of a tier, while other schools will clearly seem to be foremost in their tier, leading to the sense that there's not much breathing room between the "lowest-ranked" program in, say, tier 2, and the "highest-ranked" program in tier 3. To the extent possible, the tiers have been constructed to minimize this phenomenon—but of course it's not possible to eliminate the problem entirely. And so these "comprehensive" tiered rankings, which take into account all of the considerations listed above, should be seen as approximations, albeit the most-researched approximations possible.

Following the four tiers of rankings are two additional lists of new MFA programs. These lists may be helpful to prospective applicants trying to determine which up-and-coming schools, of the schools to which they plan to apply, are least likely to be receiving large numbers of applications (relatively speaking) during the next few application cycles. It's worth noting, given that some have expressed curiosity as to the rate of growth of MFA programs, that over the past five years an average of six new MFA programs have been created each year.

COMPREHENSIVE TIERED RANKINGS

Tier 1

Brown University
Columbia University
Cornell University
New York University
Syracuse University
University of California
  at Irvine

University of Iowa
University of Massachusetts
University of Michigan
University of Texas
University of Virginia
University of Wisconsin

Tier 2

Florida State University
Indiana University
Johns Hopkins University
University of Alabama
University of Florida
University of Houston

University of Minnesota
University of Montana
University of Notre Dame
University of Oregon
University of Washington
Washington University at
  St. Louis

Tier 3

Arizona State University
Boston University
George Mason University
Ohio State University
Pennsylvania State University
Purdue University
University of Arizona

University of Arkansas
University of Illinois
University of North Carolina
  at Greensboro
University of North Carolina
  at Wilmington
Vanderbilt University

Tier 4

Bowling Green State
  University
Brooklyn College
Colorado State University
Hollins University
Louisiana State University
The New School

Sarah Lawrence College
University of California at Davis
University of Maryland
University of Mississippi
University of Nevada at Las Vegas
University of New Mexico

On the Bubble

Hunter College [CUNY]   Western Michigan
University of Pittsburgh   University of Utah
Texas State University at San Marcos

New and Climbing*

Northwestern University   University of Massachusetts
Queens College [CUNY]   at Boston
Rutgers University at Newark University of New Hampshire
University of Colorado   University of Wyoming
University of Georgia   Virginia Tech University

Other New Programs**

Adelphi University   Rutgers University at Camden
California College of the Arts Seattle Pacific University
Fairleigh Dickinson University Southern New Hampshire
Florida Atlantic   University
Iowa State University   University of California
Long Island University   at Riverside
NEOMFA***   University of Southern Maine
New Mexico State University   Western Connecticut State
North Carolina State University   University
Pacific Lutheran University

* Date of program initiation: Queens College [CUNY], 2007; Rutgers University at Newark, 2007; University of Colorado, 2006; University of Georgia, 2006; University of Massachusetts at Boston, 2007; University of New Hampshire, 2003; University of Wyoming, 2005; Virginia Tech University, 2005; Northwestern University, 2008.

** Includes programs accepting their first classes between 2002 and 2007.

*** A consortium of four northeast Ohio schools: Cleveland State University, Kent State University, the University of Akron, and Youngstown State University.

Program Descriptions

Whatever anyone may say about any particular MFA program, it's always important to keep in mind that any MFA program—

including each of those listed below—has far more in common with its peers than could ever set it apart. So, to the extent the descriptions below seem narrowly focused on the differences between the programs, it is only because a rote listing of the countless similarities among all these programs would interest precisely no one. Likewise, it's worth stating from the outset that, whatever is said here about any of these programs—or is imputed into the descriptions of them that follow—one thing should be abundantly clear: these programs are the top programs in the country, and any student would be extremely lucky to attend any one of them. The baseline from which the following assessments begin is this: what follows are descriptions of, quite simply, the finest MFA programs anywhere in America, period. Any and all criticism of these programs (for instance, such as one might find, on occasion, below) should be taken with that in mind, and in that spirit.

In providing brief snapshots of each program, any information already available on the individual programs' websites was largely excluded, for the obvious reason that prospective students are, of course, expected to do some basic research into the various programs they're interested in on their own. And, for those students who do such Internet-based research, it will shortly become clear just how guarded most programs are with information about the nuts and bolts of their operations, and thus how elusive any brief snapshot of a program will necessarily be.

In the descriptions below, acceptance rates are sometimes referenced, and a brief note should be made on this score. First and most important, because "yield" data is not available for any MFA program in America—that is, data detailing what percentage of the candidates admitted to a given program actually decide to attend it—it's impossible to know any program's "final" acceptance rate. Consequently, all "acceptance rates" listed here are calculated by taking the number of students in a program's entering class and dividing it by the number of applications that the program was last reported to have received. The resultant figure is termed, here, a "yield-exclusive acceptance rate" because it cannot and does not take into account that some schools only occasionally "lose" an admitted candidate, while other schools have an extremely hard time getting accepted candidates to say "yes" to their offers of admission, and thus make greater use of their wait list.

Finally, it should be noted that, where cost of living for a particular town or city is noted, it is the product of a comprehensive cost-of-living study conducted in preparation for creating this ranking, one in which every college and university location relevant to this ranking was compared to a constant. In this case, the constant was a randomly selected locale: Valdosta, Georgia.

TIER 1

Brown University: Widely known as the top choice for poets and writers with an experimental bent to their writing, Brown is definitely a top ten program overall. The program matches a top-notch funding scheme with an excellent and forward-looking faculty. Nor does Brown's Ivy League status hurt; Cornell and Brown are the only Ivies offering an affordable creative writing degree, at least until Harvard, Yale, Princeton, Dartmouth, and Penn decide to initiate their own programs. Perhaps it is not surprising, then, that only two or three programs in America receive more applications per year than Brown, and that the program's acceptance rate—exclusive of yield, around 2 percent—probably ranks behind only Cornell, the University of Texas, the University of Virginia, and the University of Wisconsin. Like all of these other top programs, Brown's MFA is tiny, accepting only fourteen students (across four genres) per year. In terms of small program size, the school's ten poetry/fiction slots rank behind only Cornell and the University of Mississippi.

Columbia University: In the most literal sense, Columbia is a study in contrasts: almost certainly in the top 5 percent of all MFA programs nationally in terms of prestige, the success of its graduates, and the luster of its faculty roster, it is equally certain that Columbia is among the bottom 5 percent in its funding of students, and that this latter shortcoming now threatens to erode the long-standing reputation of the program. Certainly the fact that Columbia is one of the five largest MFA programs in America makes it unlikely that the funding situation there will be remedied overnight; no one realistically expects the program to fully or even significantly fund every one of the more than seventy students it admits each year anytime soon. That said, when the cost of living in New York City is added to the cost of attending an Ivy League institution, the fact that Columbia offers virtually no funding whatsoever to the vast majority of its students is simply a disqualifier for many prospective applicants. For those with nearly six figures' worth of available cash, however—or for those willing to go into student loan debt to a similar tune—this two-year program frankly offers very nearly the best of everything: the best location in which to be an artist, the best or near-best faculty, the best name recognition in the field after Iowa, and one of the best alumni networks going. Moreover, due to the program's near-prohibitive cost, applicants' chances of getting in aren't nearly as low as one would imagine. Unlike other top-tier programs, applicants have at worst a 10 percent chance of getting in, and possibly much higher than that if the school's potentially problematic "yield" is taken into account. The bottom line on Columbia, then, is fairly simple: if you can afford to go there without taking on a mountain of personal debt, you should go.

Cornell University: Easily a top ten program overall; no program is smaller (eight admits in two genres per year) or harder to get into (an acceptance rate hovering just over 1 percent) than Cornell. While somewhat expensive given its size, Ithaca, New York, is considered a prime location among creative writing applicants, not least because Cornell more than meets Ithaca's high cost of living with an incredible funding package. Equally strong in both poetry and fiction, Cornell can boast postgraduate successes entirely out of proportion with the miniscule size of the program itself. While the program has recently scaled back somewhat on its once-jawdropping promise of a guaranteed two-year lectureship at Cornell following graduation, the fact remains that Cornell does as much as any program in America to help students postgraduation (through an ongoing but now more modest program of awarding fully funded postgraduation positions at the university) as well as during their stay in Ithaca (through, for instance, a generous summer funding program). Perhaps not surprising, given that it is attached to one of the most prestigious—and theory-oriented—English PhD programs in America, Cornell's MFA program is also considered, in both poetry and fiction, to be particularly "theory friendly." The school's top-notch and uniformly strong faculty is headlined by poets Alice Fulton and Stephanie Vaughn. Yet perhaps the best summarization of the strength of Cornell's MFA program would be this one: it is likely the school that the most students wish to attend, even when one includes the University of Iowa.

New York University: The advice provided above regarding Columbia University could just as easily, and with equal force, apply to NYU: if you can afford to attend without going into debt, there's no reason whatsoever not to do so. New York City, and NYU in particular, is as desirable a locale as could be imagined for aspiring poets, and neither the city nor the program is any slouch when it comes to fiction, either. Almost certainly offering one of the top ten faculties in the nation, NYU is also among the most popular programs in America, routinely receiving well over 700 applications, and in at least one recent year (it is reported) over 900. That said, because NYU is one of the largest programs out there, and because it's reasonable to speculate that programs with more modest funding have lower yields, NYU carries with it a higher chance of acceptance—all things being equal—than other programs clearly within the top twenty nationally. The most recent yield-exclusive acceptance rate reported at NYU was approximately 6.5 percent, or more than three times the acceptance rate at smaller, nonmetropolitan (and same-state) programs like Cornell.

Syracuse University: For an incredibly well-regarded program with excellent funding, Syracuse's application numbers are surprisingly low, and its yield-exclusive acceptance rate surprisingly high (around 5 percent), making it an excellent target for applicants—particularly in fiction, its strongest suit reputation-wise. A program long associated with the legendary Raymond Carver still boasts a strong fiction faculty, including writers George Saunders and Christopher Kennedy. And yet the poetry faculty is as or even more stacked with stars, including well-known poets Michael Burkhard, Brooks Haxton, Mary Karr, and Bruce Smith. The overall impression one gets of Syracuse is of a program permanently entrenched in the top ten in the nation, with an across-the-board reputation for excellence. While some graduates have been known to speak ill of the program's location, Syracuse certainly receives high marks for being an inexpensive place to live, and most writers will quickly realize that Syracuse's offer of three fully funded years in which to write is incredibly valuable, regardless of the locale attached to it. In addition, the program's small size—only six students are admitted in each of poetry and fiction every year—means a greater opportunity to seek out a long-term mentor on the faculty.

University of California at Irvine: Certainly in the top five, reputation-wise, of all fiction programs nationally (and with an acceptance rate, for that genre, hovering around 2%), Irvine's poetry program is less well-known. For both genres, however, the funding is good, and the luster of the school's reputation in fiction—perhaps second only to Iowa's—is certainly a boon to the program as a whole and to all its graduates. In terms of honors and fellowships, Irvine's graduates in fiction perform as well or better than those of any other fiction program in America postgraduation, and perhaps not surprisingly the school places many graduates into the academy as well. In fact, Irvine is so well-regarded that recently the program claimed to have "lost" admitted students to another program for the very first time (for the curious, the claim was that students had been lost, in the genre of fiction, to the University of Texas). The plausibility of the "first-time-ever" claim notwithstanding, the fact remains that Irvine is beyond a shadow of a doubt the best MFA program on the West Coast—a not insignificant distinction given the importance of location to prospective MFA students' matriculation decisions. Also one of the smallest programs in the nation—with ten poets and twelve fiction writers total across two years of admittees, the larger number of fiction writers again reifying the program's emphasis on that genre—the fiction faculty at Irvine was once considered the best in America, and while not as strong now as it has been in the past, it is still excellent. Finally, given that New York City and California are the two geographic locations in America with which, as a rule, poorly funded programs may justly be associated, Irvine is a breath of fresh air—as all students receive some form of financial assistance. The same probably can't be said of any other program in either the Big Apple or Cali.

University of Iowa: For all the strong feelings—some negative—engendered by the prominent place the Iowa Writers' Workshop has long held in the MFA pantheon, one thing remains indisputable: Iowa is the oldest and most prestigious MFA program in the United States. A large program (between twenty-two and twenty-eight students are admitted in each of poetry and fiction every year), Iowa nevertheless is not simply the most well-regarded program because it's graduated more poets and writers than any other program in the country, though it. has. The simple truth is that the Workshop's record in placing graduates in academia and at the highest echelons of the publishing world is unmatched. Even more than this, the program is increasingly being recognized for its funding. Once known primarily for its tiered system of financial aid awards, Iowa has, under a new directorship, taken enormous strides to try to ensure that all students receive whatever funding they require to attend, through fellowships, scholarships, assistant-ships, and internships. While the funding is not yet uniform, each year more and more applicants are finding Iowa affordable not only because of the low cost of living in Iowa and the minimal in-state tuition for qualifying students but also because the program is in a better position than most, financially, to meet the varying financial needs of its students. Beyond this, the program has a little-publicized but extensive series of postgraduate fellowships avail-able—in fact, Iowa may well offer more postgraduate fellowships than any program in the country. Another little-known fact about Iowa is that, because of its size, its overall acceptance rate is fairly high, even though it receives far more applications than any other program in the nation (now over 1,500 applications annually). In poetry, the yield-exclusive acceptance rate is presently just under 5 percent; the fiction program, for which the school is most well-known—and which holds a much greater advantage over its next closest competitor than is the case with the poetry program—that figure is less than 3 percent. Compared to other elite programs, whose acceptance rates are well below 2 percent, Iowa is actually many applicants' best bet to be admitted to a top program, and each year stories (largely true) circulate of students being rejected outright by third- and fourth-tier schools, only to then be accepted by Iowa. Iowa's size therefore becomes, in this view, one of its most attractive assets to prospective applicants.

University of Massachusetts: Recent polls of MFA applicants sug-gest that the University of Massachusetts has become the third most popular program to apply to in America (after only the University of Iowa and the University of Michigan). And there's no mystery to that, either: long considered one of the five or six best poetry pro-grams in America (the faculty boasts James Tate, Dara Weir, and Peter Gizzi), and with countless success stories among its recent poetry graduates (including, but certainly not limited to, a Pulitzer Prize for Natasha Trethewey), the reality is that UMass is almost as strong in fiction as well. Application numbers are now soaring at UMass, with the result being a yield-exclusive acceptance rate approaching 3 percent. While the funding at UMass is only average to above average, the sense overall is that the only thing that keeps UMass from being a perennial top five stalwart is that it hasn't been performing at its current level long enough. Which means, of course, that if UMass continues to be as successful—and to draw in as many applications in the future—as it has been lately, it will be regularly mentioned in the same breath as Cornell, Virginia, Michigan, and Iowa. In poetry, it may even, one day, outstrip all five of those programs in popularity and reputation. The fact that the program is three years in duration, and is located in a college-rich environment—there are five major colleges and universities in the Amherst, Massachusetts area alone—is an added plus. Easily a top ten program overall.

University of Michigan: Without question, Michigan is one of the top three programs overall in America, and some would argue that in poetry it is presently the very best. The funding package is absolutely stunning (second only to Texas's), the overall reputation of the university impeccable, the locale beautiful, the faculty accomplished and notoriously generous with their time, and the size of the program small enough to feel cozy (twelve students admitted per year in each of poetry and fiction) but large enough to foster some significant diversity and keep the workshopping experience fresh. With a yield-exclusive acceptance rate inexplicably standing at 4 percent—the popularity of the school in recent polling suggests it will shortly be down with Brown University, Cornell University, and the universities of Wisconsin and Virginia at a 2 percent acceptance rate or below—there's simply no excuse (personal issues aside) for any prospective MFA student, in poetry or fiction, not to apply to Michigan. Should Iowa ever lose its long held place as the top creative writing MFA program overall in America, it will be to Michigan. In short, Michigan is quite nearly the perfect MFA program.

University of Texas at Austin: Given that it offers, beyond any shadow of a doubt, the best funding package of any MFA program in America, perhaps it's not surprising that Texas also receives more applications per year—approximately 800—than any program not located in Iowa City, Iowa (although New York University's fluctuating application numbers have at least once passed the 900 threshold). Located in an excellent college town, Austin, the knock against Texas, to the extent there's ever been one, has related to the structure of the program itself: the sense among students is that the program is heavily tilted toward the fiction side of things, and that the program's system of rotating visiting faculty, with no dedicated faculty members exclusively assigned to the graduate program only, short-changes students. The good news is that the program plans on soon hiring a permanent faculty member in poetry; the bad news, for all applicants, is that one's yield-exclusive chances of being admitted to the Michener Center presently stand at less than 2 percent. Once its faculty issues are finally resolved—and a permanent, MFA-only faculty put in place—Texas will be a perennial top five program. As it stands now, it's unquestionably a top ten pick.

University of Virginia: Certainly one of the top five programs overall in the nation, Virginia has one of the best faculties around and a very strong funding package. A small program—only twelve students total are admitted each year—the difference between Cornell's nation-leading selectivity and Virginia's is literally infinitesimal, and Virginia should be treated as being as difficult to get into as any program anywhere, with less than 2 percent of applicants admitted in recent years. Particularly strong in poetry, Virginia's faculty includes such luminaries as poets Rita Dove and Charles Wright, and fiction writer Deborah Eisenberg. Few programs graduate more successful writers than Virginia does, and perhaps that's something to do with the program's incredible two-to-one student-to-faculty ratio, which appears to be the best in the nation. When you add to these considerations the stellar reputation of the university as a whole, there seems to be no reason—as is the case with the University of Michigan—not to apply here. The only marks against the program, and they're both remarkably small ones, are that Charlottesville is slightly more expensive than many of the other locales that host well-funded programs, and that Virginia's excellent funding is nevertheless "only" top twenty, and not top ten, due to the minimal stipend that accompanies the tuition remission of students' first year in the program.

University of Wisconsin: The University of Wisconsin is almost certainly the biggest surprise entrant to the top tier of MFA programs. The fact is, however, that a yield-exclusive acceptance rate of

1.5 percent—coupled with soaring applications and a consistent top twenty finish in popularity polls—simply can't be ignored. Indeed, when you put together a university with a great overall reputation and a program in the top five nationally for funding (all students get full tuition remission, and an assistantship/summer funding package worth a total of more than $13,000 over twelve months) you get a program looking more and more like the University of Michigan's. In fact, within the next ten years or so, these two Midwestern programs may begin to be mentioned in the same breath. One oddity about Wisconsin that prospective applicants should be aware of: the program employs an alternating-year poetry and fiction application process, such that poets are admitted one year and fiction writers the next. While the faculty at Wisconsin isn't necessary star-studded, the program exudes that more-important sense that its professors genuinely care about admitted students; indeed, the only reason the program admits just six students each year—technically the smallest entering class of any program in America—is to ensure full and uniform funding for every accepted student. True, prospective applicants specializing in the program's "off-year" genre may grumble at missing an opportunity to apply, but frankly the program's so strong one is tempted to say that waiting might actually be worth it.

TIER 2

Florida State University: It is remarkable that a program as large as Florida State's is able to offer a competitive funding package for almost every student, and yet it does. The program receives additional luster from the fact that FSU is also home to one of the top two or three most well-regarded creative writing PhD programs in America, if not the very best. Recently named one of the top ten programs in America by a reporter for the *Atlantic*, popularity polls taken among current MFA applicants suggest that FSU is more properly seen as a top thirty program (reputation-wise) bolstered slightly by a strong funding package and the program's own aggressive self-marketing (and, moreover, its marketing of its students; the program boasts an excellent success rate for placing its graduates in tenure-track positions). While there is some basis, indeed, to wonder whether the reality of the program could possibly match the hype—and while some applicants may balk at the sheer size of the program, numbers-wise—a strong faculty (including Virgil Suarez, Erin Belieu, Julianna Baggott, Barbara Hamby, James Kimbrell, David Kirby, and Robert Olen Butler) keeps interest in the program high. And, too, the popularity of the aforementioned PhD program—particularly in poetry—does indeed add a legitimate sense of accomplishment to the entire program, making it an attractive "name" destination for young writers, particularly poets. Given that the selectivity of the program is as yet unknown—there's no data available on either the school's acceptance rate or its annual number of applications—it's hard to make any conclusive determinations about precisely where in the second tier FSU would properly be located.

Indiana University Listing the attributes of Indiana University's MFA program makes one wish that the listing of first-tier MFA programs could be twenty-five schools long instead of only twelve. Indiana has just about everything to recommend it, except an ever-so-slightly less lustrous reputation when compared to other top schools. More important, however, are the strengths of the program, which are legion: a three-year duration; the relatively low cost of living in Bloomington; a modest size (six poets and six fiction writers admitted each year); a miniscule yield-exclusive acceptance rate (less than 3 percent) but also a modest number of annual applications (perfect for MFA bargain-hunters); an excellent 3:1 student-to-faculty ratio; and, most important, full funding for all students for all three years. Indeed, every student is guaranteed an assistantship with a $12,000+ stipend and full tuition remission, and most students see their awards augmented by fellowship money, too. There's simply nothing not to like here.

The Johns Hopkins University: Once ranked the number two program in the nation, over the past ten years or so Johns Hopkins would probably have been more accurately characterized as a solid top twenty program with a strong tilt toward fiction. Indeed, up until recently the closest analogy to Johns Hopkins would have been the University of California at Irvine: in other words, a program with strong funding (in fact, at Johns Hopkins, full funding for all) and a fiction program that significantly outshines its poetry counterpart. But then JHU switched its MA format to the more popular MFA one, and in January of 2007 hired two prominent poets, Brad Leithauser and Mary Jo Salter, to join the faculty—thereby significantly increasing the viability of the poetry program and the program as a whole. While it's not entirely clear that this change has yet had a significant impact in the MFA applicant community (as many poets may not realize that the school's poetry program has recently received an infusion of new talent), one expects that in due course Johns Hopkins will once again cement a place in the high second tier or possibly even low first tier of options for prospective MFA students. In the meantime, JHU continues to draw significant interest due to its excellent funding. While the program's location is a mixed blessing—Baltimore was recently ranked one of the nation's ten most underrated cities, but is also a fairly expensive city to live in, given its size—the package at Johns Hopkins is generous enough that finances should not be a significant concern for entering students.

University of Alabama: The low cost of living in Tuscaloosa, coupled with the top-ten financial aid package offered by the program there (all students get assistantships, tuition remission, and a $10,000/year stipend), is an irresistible combination. Particularly attractive as a final destination for fiction writers—the program is easily among the top twenty fiction programs in the country, with a sub–3 percent yield-exclusive fiction acceptance rate (by comparison, it's more than 7 percent for poetry)—Alabama is also notable for the fact that it's a three-year program. While the faculty doesn't necessarily have any superstars to speak of, there's nevertheless a sense that Alabama is something of a diamond in the rough, as applicants seem more inclined to flock to high-profile programs in the Midwest and on the coasts. The truth, however, is that if you're looking to be financially secure for three years, and graduate from a school known for its solid fiction program, you should be applying to Alabama. While selectivity-related figures aren't yet available—that is, as to either acceptance rate or number of annual applications—there's reason to believe that Alabama might be a slightly more accessible admit, due primarily to its location, than other first- and second-tier programs.

University of Florida: There's a largely indefinable sense that Florida has slipped slightly since its heyday in the 1990s, but in fact the program has consistently been considered a top twenty-five school that is not, however, among the very elite programs. The school's low application figures and slightly high acceptance rate—200 people and 7.5 percent, respectively, at last accounting—are a testament to the fact that it is often overlooked by students looking to attend a high-end MFA program. It's not entirely clear what the hesitation is, however, as Florida has one of the top ten funding packages in the nation (all students get a full tuition waiver and either an assistantship or a fellowship or both, with substantial stipends attached), has recently switched to a three-year format (which enhances the value of the financial aid package significantly), and the University of Florida is, overall, one of the fastest-rising public universities in America, reputation-wise. The popular *U.S. News* ranking of undergraduate programs put the University of Florida's reputation within striking distance of the public universities of Texas, Washington, Illinois, and Wisconsin. Could it be that applicants just don't want to live in Gainesville? If so, that, too, is mystifying, as you'd be hard-pressed to find a better combination of low cost of living and a generous financial package (the proper analogy here, of course, would be Alabama's situation, described immediately above). Could the problem be the faculty? No, as the program is certainly above average in that regard. The message to applicants then, it seems, is clear: if for some reason you've been avoiding applying to the University of Florida, start applying.

University of Houston: Recently named one of America's most underrated cities, Houston is certainly one of its least expensive, significantly adding to the value of the University of Houston's already excellent funding package. At Houston, most students receive full tuition remission and an assistantship with stipend, and there are numerous fellowships available to augment student financial aid packages. Of course, funding is only one of Houston's many strengths; another primary asset is the program faculty, particularly in poetry. With Tony Hoagland, Mark Doty, Adam Zagjewski, Robert Phillips, and Nick Flynn on board, Houston easily has one of the top five poetry faculties in America. Nor can the fiction faculty, headed up by Antonya Nelson and Robert Boswell, be described as anything but extremely strong. While the program's number two ranking by *U.S. News* in 1997 no longer seems entirely dead-on, Houston's place in the top twenty MFA programs nationally is firmly established. A medium-sized program—ten poets and ten fiction writers are admitted each year—Houston is well-represented in terms of postgraduate awards, including two Stegner Fellows in 2007. Above all, however, it must be remembered that Houston is not only home to a top twenty MFA program, but also to a creative writing PhD program that is, like Florida State's, almost certainly in the top three nationally. And a lot of that can be attributed to the school's world-class faculty.

University of Minnesota: It's easy to forget that Minnesota is still a relatively young program, so young that it didn't crack the top sixty programs back when comprehensive MFA rankings were last formally released in the mid-1990s. Well, times have changed, and Minnesota is poised to move to the head of the second tier of MFA programs. With a top-notch faculty headlined by fiction-writer Charles Baxter and poets Ray Gonzalez and Patricia Hampl, and a yield-exclusive acceptance rate just north of 5 percent, Minnesota is an attractive higher-odds option for prospective MFA students determined to attend one of the top fifteen schools in the nation. While the quality of a program's location is a determination best left to applicants themselves, it's worth mentioning that Minneapolis was recently named one of the nation's most underrated cities, and that one of the primary motivations for that designation was the city's thriving arts community. Minneapolis (for those who don't mind the cold) is known as the sort of place students are loathe to leave upon graduation. A reasonable (but rising) cost of living there, coupled with the program's excellent financial package— Minnesota is one of the few programs in the nation to publicly, on its website, "guarantee" students full funding for three years— puts Minnesota no more than a hair's breadth behind programs like the University of Wisconsin, the University of California at Irvine, and the University of Massachusetts, and roughly on par with the University of Washington. In a 2008 poll of MFA applicants, Minnesota placed eleventh, and the school seems likely to hold that position or improve upon it in future years. Size-wise, Minnesota is on the low end of the midsized programs, smaller than Michigan but larger than Virginia.

University of Montana: That a program like Montana can be comfortably placed in the middle of the second tier of MFA programs is a testament, actually, to just how many stellar MFA programs there are in America. Equally strong in poetry, fiction, and nonfiction—and one of the few programs able to make that claim—Montana has just about everything you could ask for, apart from an urban location, of course: a relatively low cost of living; a shockingly approachable yield-exclusive acceptance rate (just over 10 percent); a class size right in the middle of the midsized programs; a long-standing reputation (it was ranked in the top ten of MFA programs nationally as long as a decade ago, by *U.S. News*); a consistent top twenty assessment among recent polls of prospective students; and an extremely strong faculty in both fiction and poetry (and one of the ten to twelve best in the nation, in the latter category). Critics might quibble with the funding—only half the student body can expect to get an assistantship with tuition remission and a stipend—but even in this regard, the program is merely average, not below average. Finally, while there's no scientific data to support this claim, the sense one gets is that Montana's students are among the most enthusiastic and satisfied MFA students out there. It seems that being in a small (and beautiful) college town in Montana is a strong incentive for class bonding.

University of Notre Dame: Like Alabama, a classic example of a diamond in the rough, Notre Dame amped up its funding package recently and consequently seems to have made the largest leap in popularity of any school in America over the past ten years: in 1997, *U.S. News* placed Notre Dame last—yes, last—among all the schools included in its study (more than eighty total), and now Notre Dame has cracked the top fifteen in the P&W Reader Poll and the top twenty in the Kealey/Abramson funding ranking. What a story! Particularly as, at the last public count, the program was still receiving fewer than 200 applications per year and accepting slightly more than 5 percent of them. Almost certainly those numbers have jumped and dipped, respectively, in just the few short months since they were first gathered. Poets, in particular, are flocking in large numbers to Notre Dame—not surprising given the excellence of the poetry faculty in South Bend, starting with Cornelius Eady and Joyelle McSweeney.

University of Oregon: Persistent student complaints over relations with certain faculty at Oregon are perhaps the only thing keeping this program from truly approaching top-tier status. With a yield-exclusive acceptance rate of just over 2 percent, full tuition remission

and assistantships for all students (albeit with a somewhat modest sub-$10,000 stipend), and a nice balance between small and
large, size-wise (thirteen students are admitted each year), were it
not for the seemingly high level of graduate dissatisfaction with
the program, Oregon would do battle with Indiana to supplant
Wisconsin in tier 1 of these comprehensive tiered rankings. It's not
entirely clear what would be required to clear the air over Oregon's
recent rocky history, however, so it seems that a lingering uncertainty among potential applicants will remain for some while longer. If Oregon's students were as satisfied with their program, as a
whole, as Montana's and Colorado State's, Oregon would almost
certainly be in the top ten nationally—a significant improvement
over its thirty-third place finish in the comprehensive rankings of
the mid-1990s.

University of Washington: Washington finds its way into the
second tier here not because of its funding, which is only average,
but because—like the University of California at Irvine—its reputation in one of the two "major" genres is nearly unmatched, in
this instance in the field of poetry. Boasting a faculty that includes
Heather McHugh, Andrew Feld, Linda Bierds, and Pimone
Triplett, Washington's should be considered one of the top ten
poetry faculties in America. Statistically, too, Washington would
seem like an attractive option for applicants aiming at a top program, as traditionally it has, like Florida, had among the fewest
applicants and highest acceptance rate of the programs in the top
two tiers, receiving at last count in the mid-300s for applicants and
accepting a yield-exclusive 5+ percent of them—though oddly, the
school's website describes the acceptance rate, less generously, as
being "less than 10%." While not as prestigious across the board
as Iowa, Michigan, Virginia, Cornell, or Columbia, Washington
consistently polls in the top fifteen in America in applicant popularity, and so must be considered a legitimate very-high second-
tier program.

Washington University at St. Louis: For a reliably well-funded
program widely considered one of the best in poetry in the nation,
Washington University receives an absurdly small number of applications—120 was the last publicly-observed figure—suggesting that
students are just starting to really warm to this top-notch program.
Indeed, the university has just entered the top twenty in overall

popularity (in recent two-year polling), even as it is considered, in poetry, a perennial top ten program. And what's not to like? A well above-average funding package, a university with a nationally recognized reputation in many fields, a world-class creative writing faculty (particularly in poetry, where poets Mary Jo Bang and Carl Phillips are featured), and a shockingly reasonable cost of living make Washington University, like the University of Washington, a very high second-tier option. Also, Washington University is one of the few programs, along with the University of California at Davis and Brown University, that projects as being slightly more open to experimental work than elsewhere (though perhaps less dramatically so than those other two programs). A small program—accepting fewer than ten students per year—Washington University's acceptance rate is unexpectedly high, at last count above 7 percent. Applications are undoubtedly skyrocketing, however, so young poets (in particular) are advised to move quickly.

TIER 3

Arizona State University: For several years back in the late 1990s and early part of this decade, Arizona State's star had faded slightly, largely due to funding limitations and large incoming classes—always a dangerous mix. More recently, the program has seen a significant influx of new funds, and class sizes are now slowly being drawn down. Last year's class consisted of only twelve students total (across three genres), an incoming class even smaller than Brown's, and approaching the miniscule size of Cornell's. Not surprisingly, the new ratio of funds to students at ASU has allowed the program's financial aid package to blossom, and now all incoming students receive either a research assistantship, a teaching assistantship, or a program assistantship in arts administration (with full tuition remission for any position of 50 percent time or greater) and may compete for a number of fellowships made available through the Virginia G. Piper Center for Creative Writing. One gets the sense that the program at ASU is especially geared toward attracting poets, as—and this is not necessarily as common as one might think—the program director is on the poetry faculty rather than the fiction faculty, and there are five poets but only three novelists total on the staff. ASU should now be seen as a top fifteen program in funding and a top twenty-five program in poetry, with the fiction program just a tad behind.

Boston University: Boston University is a bit of a strange duck among MFA programs. Originally an MA program, it has recently morphed into an MFA, despite retaining its most distinctive quality, a one-year duration. A medium-sized program—twelve poets, twelve fiction writers, and six playwrights are accepted each year— BU doesn't offer the best funding around, but is obviously a prime target for playwrights and certainly has one of the most illustrious creative writing faculties this side of Columbia. Still, it was something of a surprise when the *Atlantic* recently named BU one of the top ten programs nationally, as all indications, frankly, are to the contrary—and that the program, while still extremely strong, has slipped slightly (somewhat like Arizona) in general esteem over the past decade. The yield-exclusive acceptance rate is still low (4 percent), however, so it may well be that while most students are gravitating more toward longer programs than shorter ones, and fully funded programs versus those where funding is not guaranteed, there remains a strong contingent of prospective applicants looking for a high-intensity, brief-duration degree program. And for those students BU offers about as much as anyone could want (and frankly, even if it didn't, there wouldn't be any other one-year options out there). The world-class faculty at BU includes Ha Jin, Robert Pinsky, Derek Walcott, Louise Glück, and Rosanna Warren, making it one of the three or four most well-regarded poetry faculties in the nation and likely one of the six or seven most accomplished faculties overall.

George Mason University: A large program—nearly forty students are admitted every year, across three genres (poetry, fiction, and nonfiction)—George Mason's yield-exclusive acceptance rate is correspondingly high, relatively speaking (over 11 percent). Perhaps in part because, like Arizona, GMU graduates more students per year than almost any other program, the school is in select company in terms of the size of its roster of successful graduates, particularly in the field of poetry. Somewhat surprisingly, given its size, the funding at George Mason isn't terrible, though by no means can every student expect to be awarded a tuition remission–eligible assistantship. One of the few programs out there (along with Montana) considered equally strong in poetry, fiction, and nonfiction, George Mason has a stolid, workmanlike low third-tier reputation which is neither glitzy nor liable to change anytime soon—which is, if one thinks about it for a moment, both a curse and a blessing.

Ohio State University: Ohio State offers full tuition remission and assistantships to all students, and it is this move toward full funding that has launched the program well into the top fifty nationally. Somewhat comparable in reputation to Penn State, OSU, also a three-year program, has a slight edge over its neighbor, inasmuch as it seems to be a program on the rise instead of one merely holding its ground. In fact, the *Atlantic* recently named OSU one of the top five "up-and-coming" programs in America. It seems clear, too, that OSU's faculty has an edge over Penn State's, with notable poets Henri Cole, Andrew Hudgins, and Kathy Fagan on staff. Indeed, OSU's particularly strong poetry program is fueled primarily by the fact that the school boasts a top fifteen faculty in the genre. Much like other recent near-fully/fully funded additions to the top fifty programs—for instance, Purdue, Vanderbilt, and Illinois—it's not yet known what kind of staying power Ohio State will have, particularly as no information on selectivity (or even program size) is readily available. If you're one of those applicants who presumes that, where acceptance rates are concerned, no news is good news— meaning, the level of selectivity might just be low enough at OSU that the program doesn't want to broadcast it—then OSU should be one of your prime targets. All in all, OSU presents as an already strong yet still exciting program, and one that won't for much longer be as accessible as it seems to be now.

Pennsylvania State University: Confusion over its funding situation has certainly hurt Penn State over the past few years: until recently, some of the available materials regarding PSU seemed to imply that the program had only a "limited" number of assistantships available; the school's website now reflects the correct state of affairs, which is that "each student in [the] program receives financial support in the form of a [full tuition remission] teaching assistantship." That sort of guarantee—rare as it is in the MFA field—puts Penn State in the top twenty in terms of funding. By way of comparison, a program with a reputation similar to Penn State's (except slightly tilted toward poetry, as opposed to Penn State's slight fiction emphasis) would be PSU's same-state cousin the University of Pittsburgh, which narrowly failed to make the top four tiers here based upon its extremely poor funding. Yet the two programs would seem, all things being equal, to be similarly well-regarded, a circumstance that offers readers a glimpse of how quickly a bad funding situation can knock an otherwise third- or fourth-tier program out of the comprehensive rankings altogether. It's worth noting that in this year's popularity polling, Penn State was in the top twenty-five for fiction, but received nary a vote in poetry, suggesting the above-referenced slight tilt in the program—or, in the popularity of the program—toward prose. Offering a three-year course of study, Penn State lags slightly behind other top twenty-five programs in terms of the name recognition of its faculty, and has a solid but somewhat muted roster of notable graduates. In all, the sense surrounding the MFA program at Penn State is that it is a solid but unspectacular program—a little like George Mason, but with funding—noteworthy primarily due to its aid package, its relatively long history (almost twenty-five years of continuous operation), its good student-to-faculty ratio (approximately 3:1), and its duration.

Purdue University: In many respects, this entry could read "see Vanderbilt, below," and the entry for Vanderbilt could read "see Purdue, above." Purdue, like Vanderbilt, illustrates an important principle about MFA programs: a college or university with a strong overall reputation, plus a near-perfect funding package, equals instant acclaim—if not the sort of prestige that takes many years to accrue. It is impossible to chart the rise of Purdue in recent years or even months without wondering, concurrently, what would happen if a Harvard, or a Yale, or a Princeton suddenly opened its doors to a small, select, and impeccably funded MFA program. Until that happens, Purdue (and Vanderbilt) are the best examples yet of how popular an already popular school can make its MFA program with just a little influx of cash. Like a number of schools in this tiered ranking—including, most notably, Washington University, University of Illinois, and University of Notre Dame—Purdue is essentially, at this point in its history, a low-application, low-admit school (the last reported numbers in fiction had the program accepting four students out of a hundred applicants in the genre). And yet, as with the other schools mentioned here, that's almost certain to change, and soon. The fact that Lafayette, Indiana, is an extremely inexpensive place to live, and that the program is three years in duration, only further highlights the impressiveness of Purdue's aid package (assistantships, full tuition remission, and a $12,000+ stipend for all admits).

University of Arizona: Arizona's allure has diminished somewhat since those heady days when *U.S. News* ranked it in the top ten, but there's no denying the fact that the program continues to excel in the areas of name recognition and producing award-winning graduates. While the funding package offered by the program is only average or slightly above, prospective students can take some comfort in the fact that no high-tier program offers such reasonable odds of admission: with an entering class more than fifty strong, and applications hovering in the mid-300s, current estimates place the program's yield-exclusive acceptance rate at upwards of 15 percent. Still long odds, to be sure, but in the creative writing field surprisingly palatable. With many more novelists and nonfiction professors than poets on staff, one gets the sense that Arizona is tilted more toward fiction and nonfiction—and is particularly favored by such applicants—in much the same way one senses at Arizona State (see above) a slighter stronger focus being applied to poetry. Still, the program as a whole does extremely well in terms of postgraduate assessments—for both genres—with Arizona-affiliated poets winning the Yale Younger Poets prize in 2002, 2003, and 2004, and several graduates receiving Stegner Fellowships (in poetry) since the mid-1990s. Along with its more than thirty-year history, the fact that Arizona has had a series of high-profile fiction graduates and places a slightly higher-than-average number of graduates into high-profile teaching positions keeps the school in the high-tier category despite its funding limitations, large size, and (relatively speaking) low selectivity.

University of Arkansas: One of the oldest creative writing MFAs, Arkansas is a well-funded three-year program. It also has the additional benefit of being located in Fayetteville, the second-cheapest place to live of all the towns and cities analyzed for this tiered ranking. Moreover, with two excellent young poets on the faculty—Davis McCombs and Geoffrey Brock—balanced nicely by a number of veteran poets and writers, the program's already excellent just over three-to-one student-to-faculty ratio seems especially enticing. For such a small program, Arkansas's list of prominent graduates is impressive, particularly in poetry: Adam Clay, Chelsea Rathburn, Tony Tost, Beth Ann Fennelly, Al Maginnes, Gordon Grice, R. S. Gwynn, and C. D. Wright are all Arkansas graduates. Arkansas has also had a particularly fine track record in placing graduates into academia and prestigious fellowships, such as the Stegner Fellowship at Stanford. Despite all its allure, however, Arkansas still receives relatively few applications for a high-tier school—250, at last count—and its roughly 4 percent yield-exclusive acceptance rate makes it a highly competitive but still somewhat more accessible alternative to more selective well-funded programs such as those at the University of Oregon, University of Wisconsin, and Indiana University. Finally, it's worth noting that Arkansas was recently named one of the top five most innovative MFA programs by the *Atlantic*, a designation that's sure to cause applications to jump in upcoming cycles.

University of Illinois: A fast-rising program, whose last publicly reported number of applications was a head-scratching sixty-two—with four acceptances—Illinois nevertheless enters now into the top tiers of creative writing programs because of its excellent funding package and the overall reputation of the school, certainly one of the top public institutions in the nation. Which is not to suggest that the program's faculty is any slouch, either, as in fact it's quite the opposite: with a relatively young group of poets and writers on staff, including Brigit Pegeen Kelly and Tyehimba Jess in poetry and Philip Graham in fiction, Illinois can boast not only an excellent student-to-faculty ratio but also a talented group of instructors. Because application numbers are still low relative to other rising programs, Illinois remains an extremely attractive option for students searching for a high-tier, (relatively) high-odds application target. As with Purdue and Vanderbilt, Illinois is a sort of poster child for the premise that, when a school with a nationally recognized English undergraduate/graduate department finally votes to initiate an MFA program—and if they also vote to fund it properly—it will eventually become extremely popular among applicants. Despite its low application numbers (that sixty-two figure has probably increased, but it could only have increased so much), recent polling suggests that Illinois has become one of the top thirty most popular programs over the past two application cycles, despite not placing in the top sixty in the rankings of ten years ago. The fact that the program is three years in duration, and funds almost all its students reliably during that time span, is an added bonus.

University of North Carolina at Greensboro: Smaller and more selective than the University of North Carolina at Wilmington—accepting a class of eleven each year overall, with an approximately 4.5% yield-exclusive acceptance rate—Greensboro is also one of the oldest MFA programs in the country, and boasts former faculty and students who have helped form the mainstream of American writing (including Allen Tate, John Crowe Ransom, and Randall Jarrell). From this depiction, students can deduce that Greensboro is harder to get into than its UNC cousin, but also less innovative, and more established in its reputation, as opposed to a young upstart. The faculty is among the best of all the MFA programs in the South, including an especially strong poetry faculty, featuring such writers as Stuart Dischell, David Roderick, and Jennifer Grotz. Overall, the impression one gets of the University of North Carolina at Greensboro is that it is aesthetically fairly conservative, and is an excellent target for prospective applicants looking for a well-established mainstream program in the South. Consistent with the fact that Greensboro is older and more established than Wilmington is the fact that Greensboro seems to offer better funding, too, including more assistantships (and with a higher stipend) than Wilmington does.

University of North Carolina at Wilmington: The number of MFA programs known for their innovative approach to the study of creative writing can be counted on one hand, so Wilmington stands out particularly in this respect. Recently named one of the top five most innovative MFA programs by the *Atlantic*—a distinction which merely confirmed existing buzz surrounding the school—Wilmington boasts a number of novel approaches in its program: for instance, a "Writers' Week" during which normal classes are canceled and students engage in intensive one-on-one manuscript conferences and other highly focused workshops/readings; an incredibly robust visiting faculty system (in just the past few years, Gerald Stern, Z. Z. Packer, Mark Doty, and the late Robert Creeley all taught at Wilmington); an absolutely top-notch nonfiction program; a strong belief in cross-genre study (including an "out-of-genre" course requirement), and an offering of courses in editing and publishing. Under some circumstances, the program even allows students to take more than one workshop per semester. Despite its size (the program admits more than twenty students per year total), the large faculty allows the program to retain a strong student-to-faculty ratio of 3:1. Indeed, size-wise Wilmington is one of the fastest-growing MFAs nationally, increasing the size of its faculty by nearly 500% (from three professors to fourteen) since its founding just eight years ago. Meanwhile, one of the benefits of the larger program size is a remarkably reasonable acceptance rate for the field, a yield-exclusive 8.4% at last reckoning. While the funding is only average—less than half of the student body is able to get teaching assistantships—the program's three-year duration means that for two-thirds of a student's time there he or she may well be eligible for the school's less-than-$5000/year in-state tuition.

Vanderbilt University: The program at Vanderbilt is yet another exemplar of the long-standing principle already twice stated, but in fact important enough to reiterate a final time: when a nationally renowned university decides to switch from partial funding to full funding for all its MFA students, that program is immediately swamped by applications and widespread interest among prospective applicants. Perhaps no program is as clear and concise about its financial aid offerings as Vanderbilt, a fact that students struggling to figure out exactly what all the other programs can offer will certainly appreciate. At Vandy, the first-year package includes a full tuition waiver, a $9,250 stipend/salary for assisting with the program's writing studio, and full health insurance (a value of approximately $2,000). Given the extremely low cost of living in Nashville, the package is excellent, especially considering that the program also offers some students, above and beyond the package described, "topping-up" awards in the form of additional fellowships. In the second year, students receive the same package, but are now asked to teach a single creative writing workshop for one semester—one of the most minimal teaching requirements attached to a stipend in the entire nation. Plus, students are allowed to retain in subsequent years any annual fellowship awards issued in their first year, which takes all the worry and uncertainty out of the financial aid process; at most other schools, fellowship awards are reviewed on an annual basis. Contrarian applicants may well ask whether Vanderbilt has more to offer than its stunning financial aid package and its good name, and the truth is, these do seem to be the program's two strongest attributes—and yet, these attributes are enough to place Vanderbilt in the top ten nationally in funding, and to carry the program into the top thirty of the 2008 P&W Reader Poll, the first poll to reflect the school's amendment of its financial aid package. While it may take a few more years for the program to build up its overall reputation—as with many other up-and-coming programs, Vanderbilt was not listed at all in the 1997 *U.S. News* rankings—the near certainty of increased applications associated with its funding package is bound to have a significant impact on the program's prestige over time. And with only twelve students accepted each year, it seems likely that Vanderbilt will be able to be extremely selective about who it takes going forward.

TIER 4

Bowling Green State University: It's become extremely popular to describe BGSU as an up-and-coming program—and indeed it's fought its way into the top forty in the P&W Reader Poll, no easy task—but the reality is that the program, as one of the oldest of its kind in the nation, has been graduating successful poets and writers for years, and perhaps is only just now getting its proper due (in the rankings of programs done in 1997, it failed to crack the top seventy). Located in a relatively inexpensive area of Ohio, Bowling Green offers a good number of full tuition remission-eligible assistantships to students, in fact enough to earn it top fifty status in the Kealey/Abramson Funding Ranking. A low-application, low-admit program—at last count it had ten spots for less than 100 applicants, a more than 13% yield-exclusive acceptance rate—BGSU nevertheless has graduated a surprisingly large roster of successful poets and writers over the years, including Carolyn Forché, Dara Wier, Anne Panning, June Spence, and Tony Ardizzone, as well as rising stars such as F. Daniel Rzicznek and Jeanine Hathaway. The faculty at BGSU has a strong reputation for active engagement with its students, and the sense with BGSU is that it is a program that not only genuinely cares about but truly celebrates its graduates. Similar programs, as to this last feature, include the University of Montana and Colorado State University.

Brooklyn College: The financial aid package at Brooklyn is, typical for the area, fairly limited. That said, the program's costs are significantly less than its Manhattan counterparts: $500 per credit for nonresidents of New York, and $270 per credit for residents. The program received recognition recently by the *Atlantic*, which named it one of the top five "up-and-coming" programs in America. The honor certainly seems deserved, especially considering the strong desire for prospective creative writing students to find a moderately affordable alternative, in New York City, to NYU and Columbia. Fiction-writers should be especially attracted to Brooklyn, as it boasts a strong faculty in the genre, including Michael Cunningham and Myla Goldberg. The allure of a less-expensive New York City–based alternative to the better-known programs has not gone unnoticed by applicants, however: the yield-exclusive acceptance rate at Brooklyn is less than 10%, making it a more difficult admit these days, ironically, than Columbia.

Colorado State University: CSU is an excellent program—just ask its students. Along with Montana and Bowling Green, CSU presents as having an especially high satisfaction rate among its graduating classes. In most other respects, Colorado State presents as average to above-average: a cost of living somewhere in the middle of all the locales assessed; a funding system that's above average, but just barely in the top forty (nothing to sneeze at, of course); an above-average faculty; the opportunity for three years of study as opposed to two; an as-yet-unreported acceptance rate; a class size that seems fairly standard; and so on. So what puts CSU in the top fifty, and into the fourth tier of this assessment? Well, beyond the fact that a program with multiple above-average indicators is without question to be admired, there's the fact that Fort Collins is an award-winning city just an hour from Denver (and even closer to some excellent skiing, if you're so inclined), and that, put bluntly, one senses at CSU a genuine commitment to the students. That sounds pretty basic, but in fact of all the programs assessed, the enthusiasm of CSU's MFA students for their program—and vice versa—was more evident than at any other school. And that definitely counts for something. To read about CSU (both in the program's sponsored materials, as well as in the materials produced by its students) is to want desperately to attend the program. Few programs are able to make such a strong impression purely through their public presence online (and through vocal recommendations from their students).

Hollins University: Hollins is a close call, so far as appearing in the top tiers is concerned—not because the program hasn't historically performed well in polls (twentieth in the mid-1990s polling, twenty-fifth in 2008 polling), but because so much uncertainty has surrounded the school in recent years. Formerly called "Hollins College," the school recently re-upped as a university; formerly an MA, the program is now an MFA; formerly one year, it's now two. The problem is that these changes didn't come without a price— or controversy. Many on the faculty at the time of the program's switch to an MFA objected, claiming the switch wouldn't allow the school to meet its financial responsibilities to students. Motives were questioned, accusations hurled, and one faculty member even threatened to resign. Still, all that said, the following facts remain true: nothing that's happened over the past decade has pushed Hollins out of the top twenty-five in popularity among students; the school boasts one of the better nonfiction programs around; Roanoke, Virginia, is cheaper than cheap (the fourth cheapest location in this assessment); and few programs can boast a more impressive roster of alumni (Annie Dillard, Henry Taylor, Madison Smartt Bell, Natasha Trethewey, and Mary Ruefle, among them). And yet, as some feared, the switch to an MFA did affect Hollins's funding, and until recently it's a crapshoot as to what kind of financial aid offers students will get (the school has recently added two fully-funded spots) And the application numbers tell the story: as much as students seem to respect Hollins's history, applications are still stuck around 200 at last count, with a yield-exclusive acceptance rate (7 percent) not particularly consistent with a top twenty-five program. All things considered, Hollins currently looks like a program slightly out of fashion; given the august history of the program, however, a significant rebound certainly isn't out of the question, particularly as the traumas of the last five years recede into the past. To its credit, Hollins offers an impressive panoply of genre options (including screenwriting, playwriting, and children's literature), so it gets the nod for the fourth tier.

Louisiana State University: Of the fewer than twenty programs nationally that prominently advertise their uniform full-funding packages, LSU may have gotten the least acknowledgment for it among applicants, and it's not entirely clear why. An extremely small program numbers-wise, nevertheless, unlike most poetry/fiction–only programs, LSU not only offers specializations in screenwriting, playwriting, and nonfiction, but also actively encourages students to take classes outside their areas of focus. Needless to say, given the size of the program the student-to-faculty ratio is excellent; moreover, LSU gets substantial credit for not merely offering students guaranteed funding but also for offering such funding in the context of a three- rather than a two-year program. One possible explanation for LSU being overlooked is the fact that it did not appear in the much-vaunted, now outdated *U.S. News* rankings of 1997, effectively keeping it off the radar screen of countless prospective applicants. Given its excellent funding, three-year duration, and presumed off-the-radar status (important for applicants looking to find fully funded programs with reasonable acceptance rates), LSU shouldn't remain much of a secret much longer. As to funding, all students get tuition remission, health insurance, an assistantship, and an unspecified stipend (not to mention a light teaching load commensurate with Vanderbilt's).

The New School: It's easy to sound like a broken record in describing MFA programs in New York City, largely because many of the same things can be said for all of the top programs in the Big Apple. And indeed, all of those same observations apply to the New School as well, as it—like its neighbors NYU and Columbia—offers a top-notch location for an aspiring artist, complicated somewhat by that location having the highest cost of living in America; extremely limited funding; a strong nonfiction program; an excellent faculty across all genres (but particularly strong in poetry, with such writers as David Lehman, Paul Violi, Susan Wheeler, Maggie Nelson, and Elaine Equi on staff); an enormous incoming class; a near-unparalleled number of applications per year (well over 700); a surprisingly reasonable acceptance rate (over 10 percent) and likely a sizable accompanying yield problem; and finally (as certainly bears repeating) virtually no funding available to admitted students. As with Columbia and NYU, there's nothing not to like about the New School, except the fact that too few students can afford to attend it. Still, for a relatively new program, the New School's sudden and assertive arrival on the creative writing scene has certainly been impressive—especially, as noted, on the poetry end of things—and given several more years to mature (for indeed, any school that did not appear in the 1997 *U.S. News* ranking has been at a real disadvantage since then), it seems likely that the New School will join Columbia and NYU to form a powerhouse triumvirate of incredible but essentially unaffordable MFA programs in New York City.

Sarah Lawrence College: Sarah Lawrence is a strongly poetry-tilted program, in fact one of the best in that genre. The poetry faculty is easily in the top five nationally—may even be the best in America—and includes Vijay Seshadri, Stephen Dobyns, Thomas Sayers Ellis, Matthea Harvey, Cathy Park Hong, Marie Howe, Thomas Lux, Jeffery McDaniel, D. Nurske, and Martha Rhodes. The problem, per usual for programs located in the New York City area, is poor funding, an issue grave enough at Sarah Lawrence (and, to return to a recurring theme in these descriptions, at NYU, Columbia, and elsewhere in the metropolis) that the program seems to have lately been pushed out of the top twenty-five programs overall. Still, assuming an applicant with sufficient funds, it bears emphasizing that the poetry program is in the top ten, the location can't be beat (or, as a cynic might say, afforded), and the program as a whole has an obvious and abiding commitment to frequent faculty-student interaction, requiring biweekly one-on-one conferences between students and their teachers. This commitment is especially notable because few other programs, if any, have made such conferences not merely an option but a primary feature of the program's internal structure. As with most of the other New York City–area schools, Sarah Lawrence also has a well-regarded nonfiction program.

University of California at Davis: The only MA program listed in the comprehensive tiered rankings, one of the two primary weaknesses of UCD is precisely that: it doesn't offer its students a terminal degree. The other weakness is, in fairness to UCD, one that is exceedingly common among programs in California, just as it is among programs in New York City—somewhat limited funding. And yet UCD's funding situation isn't nearly as dire as most other

California/NYC programs, and the program is to be credited with doing more than most to ensure that nearly all students can afford to attend. As to the terminal-degree issue, it seems clear that UCD is aware of this possible knock against it, as the program's website hastens to note (somewhat defensively, and not entirely accurately) that the terminal degree in the field of creative writing is actually the PhD. Prospective applicants to UCD should be aware that while this may someday be the case, it is not now, and MFA graduates are far more likely than MA graduates to earn tenure-track positions, as they can claim to have a terminal degree in their chosen field. Still, UCD appears in the tiered rankings for a reason—namely, that students looking for an MA rather than an MFA (i.e., an academic degree rather than an art degree) couldn't do much better than UCD, particularly students who know in advance they'll be going on to attend a PhD program anyway. Indeed, UCD, unlike a studio program, requires courses in theory, one workshop at a minimum outside the student's area of specialization, and at least three courses in literature. The program also boasts an excellent faculty, an especially appetizing trait in a program with a student-to-faculty ratio of less than 3:1. On the staff are both noted poets (Joshua Clover, Joe Wenderoth, and Sandra McPherson, the last of whom spent many years teaching at the University of Iowa) and highly-regarded writers (including Lynn Freed and Pam Houston). As is the case with Brown University, there is a sense with UCD that diversity in aesthetics is actively encouraged, and that "experimental" writers of poetry and prose will feel more comfortable here than perhaps they would elsewhere.

University of Maryland: Despite a less-than-stellar financial aid scheme, the University of Maryland continues to perform well in polling among prospective applicants because, put simply, its graduates do extremely well following graduation. The school ranks high in placing its graduates in academia and sending them on to fellowship- and award-winning careers in both poetry and fiction. The well-regarded faculty is also an obvious plus: among the notable professors at Maryland are poets Stanley Plumly, Elizabeth Arnold, Michael Collier, and Joshua Weiner, as well as novelist Howard Norman. Still, the financial aid package is singularly disappointing, offering students only a "limited number" of fellowships and teaching assistantships. Most students will find themselves trying to get in-state tuition rates if at all possible. While Maryland does not have a proper nonfiction program, students are encouraged to take the creative nonfiction workshop offered by the program once per year in the spring. A good way to think of Maryland would be one as either Penn State with far worse funding but a far better post-graduate track record, or, alternatively, George Mason with slightly worse funding and a slightly better postgraduate track record.

University of Mississippi: A relatively new program, Mississippi is one of the smallest MFAs in the nation—accepting only four students in poetry and four in fiction each year—and also, perhaps not coincidentally, one of the top forty best-funded. It doesn't hurt, either, that the cost of living in Oxford is extremely low, and that the university offers students three years to write instead of the usual two. Location and duration aside, the program simply has an exceptional slate of fellowships and assistantships available to its small cadre of incoming poets and writers, with each fellowship and assistantship carrying full tuition remission and a moderate to large stipend. It appears that most students can expect to receive significant or even full funding, though such funding is not guaranteed. Prospective students should note that the school does have a foreign language requirement: by the end of their two years in Oxford, students must be able to exhibit proficiency in Greek, Latin, Spanish, French, German, or Italian.

University of Nevada at Las Vegas: When the *Atlantic* recently named UNLV one of the most innovative programs in the United States, few were surprised. UNLV has consistently done more than just about any other MFA program to innovate, offering its students not only a top twenty-five funding package (with more than two dozen remission-eligible assistantships available), and not only a three-year residency, but also the opportunity to do funded study abroad. As stated on the program's excellent website, "students admitted to the MFA at UNLV follow a three-year program where students take literature and writing courses, complete a manuscript of poems or fiction, spend time abroad, and complete a translation. In addition, the MFA program at UNLV is the only creative writing program in the country that gives credit to students who wish to spend their time abroad in the Peace Corps. . . ." It's impossible not to admire UNLV's international focus, as well as its recognition that (again from the website) "the best writing is done by individuals who know that literature is something created from more than self-expression; that great books are written by the few who know their gift is connected to the world they live in, from a desire to give something back to the world." The fact that UNLV also plays host to a top creative writing PhD program doesn't hurt, either. Students looking to do more than just sit in a classroom should have UNLV at the top of their list.

University of New Mexico: An extremely young program, New Mexico gets the nod here because it's a three-year program with above-average funding and its success in such a relatively short period of time bodes well for its future. Nevertheless, its inclusion here was a down-to-the-wire decision, as competition for the final spot in the comprehensive tiered rankings was fierce; also competing for a spot in the fourth tier were Southern Illinois (which has a better funding package than New Mexico and a better student-to-faculty ratio, but much less buzz), the University of Pittsburgh (which has a much poorer funding package than either New Mexico or Southern Illinois, but a stronger and more long-standing reputation than either, and is located in one of the lowest-cost cities analyzed for these rankings), and Western Michigan University (a veteran program whose continued popularity among poets, and reputation as a strong program for poetry, makes it an obvious higher-odds target for poets everywhere). Ultimately, however, the student-friendly structure of New Mexico's program, its duration (coupled with above-average funding), and the general sense that it is a program on the verge of a notable leap forward in reputation and popularity place it just a hair ahead of these other three schools. The fact that New Mexico is a large program is of course a mixed blessing for students; and yet, the fact that New Mexico will be sending so many graduates out into the field in the coming years also gives the program more of an opportunity to make a mark in publishing and the academy. Even so, the reality is that students strapped for cash should take a harder look at Southern Illinois than UNM, that students concerned primarily about reputation should opt for Pittsburgh over UNM, and poets looking for a program that caters particularly to their needs—and, increasingly, is particularly well-regarded in their field—should look first to Western Michigan.

❧

Non-MFA Fellowship Program:

Stanford University (*written by Tom Kealey*): The Stegner Fellowship program is a two-year nondegree program in fiction or poetry, and is often thought of as a post-MFA program. Students without masters degrees have been accepted, though the main pool of applicants are students who are completing their graduate work. (I was a Stegner Fellow from 2001 to 2003). "Stegners" take six workshops on the quarter system in two years, and they can also take almost any other course offered at Stanford. Stegners can also teach in the Levinthal Tutorials, a one-on-one program with Stanford under-graduates. The fellowship offers that greatest of gifts—time; time to write and complete a book or manuscript. Stanford is in Palo Alto, California, though many fellows live in San Francisco and other Bay Area cities. Fully funded, with the additional opportunity for teaching assistantships in English department classes. Highly selective. Five poets and five fiction writers are selected from a pool of more than 1,200. I loved my time at Stanford, and I'd highly recommend the Stegner program to advanced writers.

❧

PhD and Low-Residency MFA Programs:
Some of the more distinguished PhD programs include the University of Southern California, the University of Houston, University of Missouri–Columbia, University of Utah, Florida State University, Cornell University, and the University of Nevada–Las Vegas. Meanwhile, some of the more distinguished low-residency programs include Antioch University, Bennington College, Lesley University, New Orleans University, Vermont College, and Warren Wilson College.

A Note to Program Directors

> **Johanna Foster is a graduate student in the creative writing program at Trinity College in Dublin, Ireland.**
>
> **Q:** What were your experiences with program websites?
> **A:** "Some websites indicate 'We're friendly. Here's the information. If you have questions, let us know,' others seem to say "It's really hard to get into our program. You probably won't make the cut." And a lot of them seem to say 'We don't really care about you or about designing a helpful website.'. . . This was really frustrating, because if you called a program, often the person on the line would indicate, 'You should know more about our program before you call,' but then there's not helpful information on the website. Where am I supposed to get this information?"

Seth and I are probably the only people on this planet to have visited and explored the websites of every MFA, MA, and PhD creative writing program in the country. That's around 300 websites, and it was not the easiest of experiences. If I had to hand out grades, there would certainly be a few A's and B+'s, but overall I'd put the median grade at around a D+. My goal in this short chapter is to urge program directors to push their website grades up to the B range.

If you feel like your program was misrepresented or misinterpreted in the previous brief profiles or the appendix D information, then you are welcome to lodge a complaint. My e-mail address is easily found on the Internet. You are also welcome to place some energies and resources into your program's website, as that is the primary means of relaying vital information to prospective students. A poorly designed website is often interpreted as evidence of a poorly designed creative writing program. A website need not be fancy or flashy, but information should be clearly stated and found. If you care for advice, your website should contain the following information in an easily navigated site:

Admissions—What materials, specifically and easily summarized, are required for admission to the program? What is the due date? How many students are accepted out of, approximately, how many applications? An application should be online or easily downloadable in PDF and Word formats.

About the Program—How many current students are in the program? Offer a sample schedule for your one-, two-, or three-year program. How many classes are students expected to take during which years?

Course Work—First and foremost: How many credit hours are required for the degree, and what classes are offered? Second, if there is flexibility in taking courses outside of the department, this fact should be noted. Often students like to take courses that will teach them about their particular writing interests, and these could range from biology to photography to political science.

Funding—If you feel like you provide solid funding for your graduate students, then state the specifics. What percentage of students are funded fully, and partially? Specifically, how many teaching and other fellowships are available?

Location—A few words about your city, town, or other locality is welcomed. Yes, this information is often available on the university's main website. So, why not at least copy this information on to the program's website or provide a link?

Faculty—Most sites are pretty good about this. A list of faculty and their experience and publications is appreciated. If they have creative work posted on the Internet, then I'd encourage you to link to it.

Alumni—If your past students have had some success in the publishing or academic world, do you know about it, and if so, why aren't you bragging about it? Prospective students are interested in this information. If you are interested in your alumni, then this is a good sign that you are interested in your current students.

History—Every program, even a beginning one, has a history. Students are interested in what they will be a part of. Don't be afraid to tell a story, even a brief one.

Opportunities—Is your program connected with a literary magazine or university press? State this, and provide a link. And, if there are opportunities for experience, paid or unpaid, for your graduate students, then state what those are. Some programs host summer conferences, readings in high schools, or other community outreaches. Make your prospective current students aware of these events.

Readings—Yes, a list of past visiting writers is a good thing. A list of this year's writers is even better. How many visiting writers does your program host a year? Do you also host publishers, agents, and editors, small or large? Make this information available.

Current and Recent Students—It's nice to profile your faculty. It's even nicer to profile and celebrate your current students. A brief bio, and even a photo, of current graduate students goes a long way toward making them feel valued and appreciated. And, it speaks volumes to prospective students.

Resources—This is an important aspect of program websites that, to my mind, is often lacking. What university resources are available in the areas of child care, diversity, housing, libraries, and even parking? A page of links in these areas, and others, is greatly appreciated.

Contact—The e-mail address of an individual who can answer questions is most welcome and appreciated.

Awards—Does your program offer any? If so, describe them and list past winners.

Program News—What's happening *now?* What is the latest information about opportunities, awards, publications, events, and changes in the program? This page need not be updated daily. Once a month is enough and appreciated.

Events—When and where will readings, colloquiums, and other events take place? This is as important to current students as it is to prospective students.

This advice might seem overwhelming, but that shouldn't at all be the case. The main criteria for a well-designed site is the actual information. Your department likely has a technology person on staff, and if not, your students are likely Net-savvy. Why not offer one or two of them degree credit and/or a small stipend for posting and maintaining the site? Either way, it's important to involve students, as they will more clearly see what information is needed and how it should be presented in a clear way. Want a model? Check out the University of Indiana's MFA website; the address is http://www.indiana.edu/~mfawrite/.

CHAPTER 4

The Application Process

George Saunders is a professor of creative writing at Syracuse University, where he was also an MFA student in fiction. His works include *Pastoralia* and *CivilWarLand in Bad Decline*.

Q: How does the selection committee make its decisions?
A: "Honestly, as a committee of three or four people we find we are choosing the same top fifteen applicants about 90% of the time. Our individual writing aesthetic doesn't seem to enter it to it much, by which I mean 'realist,' or 'experimentalist,' etc. What we're looking for is some combination of intelligence and reader awareness. The writer knows the effect that he or she is shooting for, and they get it. . . . As for choosing the final six students, it's a gut thing. We talk and think about who we would be excited to work with. If I find myself thinking, 'Well, I can't exactly think of a reason to reject this person,' then that basically constitutes a rejection. At our acceptance rate, I really have to feel, 'Wow, I want to talk with this person about their work. I'm excited about this work.'"

Most deadlines for applications to creative writing graduate schools fall between the beginning of December and the middle of February. The vast majority land in January. Make sure you know the deadlines for your schools, and stick to them. If you want to pay FedEx a lot of money for overnight shipping, by all means wait till the last minute. Otherwise, be sure to send your applications a week in advance. Do note that there is no real advantage to sending your applications in extremely early, though there is no drawback either.

As I've said before, an application for graduate programs will contain some of combination of:

- The writing sample. About 25–30 pages of prose or around 10–15 pages of poetry.
- Three letters of recommendation.
- A personal statement.
- Undergraduate and continuing studies transcripts.
- GRE scores.
- The actual application form itself.
- An application fee ($50–70 dollars).

And for PhD programs, many MA programs, and some MFA programs:

- A critical essay.
- GRE Literature subject scores.

One of the first things you'll want to do is make a chart, listing what materials are due to which schools. If you have an incredibly organized mind, then you can skip this step. For the rest of us, your chart will look something like . . .

Materials	School One	School Two	School Three	School Four
Deadline	December 15th	January 10th	January 15th	February 1st
Writing Sample	yes	yes	yes	yes
Letters of Recommendation	three	three	two	three
Personal Statement	yes	yes, along with teaching philosophy statement	yes	yes
GRE Scores	no	yes	yes	yes
Undergraduate (and other) Transcripts	yes, to be sent directly to the program office	yes, include in application packet	yes, either	yes, either
Application	yes	yes	yes, plus two copies	yes
Fee	$45	$50	$40	$55
Other	reading list	none	critical essay	none

As I've also said before, I am highly recommending that you apply to eight to twelve graduate programs. Why? Because programs receive around 100 to 400 applications each year, and they accept around 5% to 15% of those applications. Don't let that discourage you. Believe in your writing. But spread your net wide, and keep your options open.

I recommend that you start your application process about two months in advance. Though, that's assuming that you've been working on your writing sample long before you even knew it might *turn in* to a writing sample. Two months is especially relevant when asking for letters of recommendation. And for studying for, and completing, the GRE. If you've got less than two months, you're not sunk yet, but it's time to get in gear.

In chapter 4A, I'll include a checklist of activities you'll need to complete. For now, let's dive into the Q&A about the materials in the application.

In actual work hours, how long will the application process take?
If you apply to eight to twelve schools, and not counting the writing sample or studying for the GRE, I'd say about 30 to 40 hours. If you have the luxury, spread this time out. Work for a few hours, say, each Tuesday and Thursday night, plus Saturday mornings. Don't burn yourself out.

Keep in mind that the first application is the hardest. After that, you are reusing many of the same materials. The process becomes easier for each additional application.

How important is the writing sample?
There are many parts of this book that will cause disagreement (and I hope discussion) among writers, program directors, and professors. But one aspect that all interested parties will agree on: the writing sample is the most important element of your application. How important? It's the first thing committee members read, and if it doesn't measure up to their standards, your letters of recommendation, personal statement, transcripts, and GRE scores are completely irrelevant. If a committee receives 300 applications from which they will choose 18 students, then your writing sample will get you from the 300 level to the final 30 level. And it can quite possibly make you a lock for acceptance.

The writing sample is weighted around 90% of total importance to the application. Is it intimidating, trying to get from the 300 applicants to the final 18? Sure it is. But that's why you're spreading your net wide, applying to eight to twelve schools. And also, you believe in your work. It's quality work, and you need to put it out there.

Programs will want twenty to thirty pages of fiction or nonfiction, or about fifteen pages of poetry.

Geoffrey Wolff is the director of the graduate fiction program at the University of California–Irvine. His works include *The Art of Burning Bridges*, *The Duke of Deception*, and *The Age of Consent*

Q: What is the committee's process for considering the applications?

A: "Our deadline is January 15th, and we have to make our selections by the second week in March. Michelle Latiolais and I read all the applications. We go first to the fiction submissions. If one story seems uninteresting, we try the other story. If there's nothing there, if it's flat on the page, no music, no surprises, we don't go any farther. All the rest—gorgeous transcripts, endorsements, heart-stirring ambition—won't matter at that point. What we're looking for is difficult to articulate but not to recognize. Conventional writing about conventional wisdom is not going to claim any choosy reader's attention."

Should I anticipate what kind of "aesthetic" each program prefers?

Others will disagree with this, but my answer is a definite no. Some programs may be known for postmodern work, others for "experimental," others for "traditional." Attempting to define these terms is asking for a big headache. You can't predict which professors will be the primary readers in a particular year of applications. Sometimes all the professors read the work, sometimes it's only one or two. Some programs use outside readers. Attempting to guess the preferred aesthetic of your readers is like attempting to guess what your opponent will do in a sporting event. It has its advantages, but in the end you should be concentrating on what you're going to do. Put your best work forward. At the end of the selection process, committee members are looking for quality first, aesthetic a very distant second.

So, how do I choose my "best work"?

Your best work is likely writing that you have put a lot of time into, and it's work that has received feedback in a writing workshop or from other writers. It's polished work. It's writing that you have worked hard on, set aside, come back to, edited and expanded, deepened and clarified.

Keep in mind that you are not always the best judge of your own work. Before you send in your application you should have two or three people read your writing sample "nominees." If you have twelve poems and need to choose eight, then give your work to people you trust, and get their opinion about which work is strongest. Same thing if you have four stories and need to choose two. Who should you ask? Writing teachers, definitely. Other writers that you know are another good source. But don't rule out non-writers who are good readers. People know quality work when they see it. At least most people do. Who do you know who is well-read? Who will give you an honest opinion? Your writing teacher from your undergraduate studies is an excellent candidate, but your roommate might very well be another. Your mom or dad might be of help to you in this case, but I'd doubt it. Let your mom or dad help you out in other areas of your life. I hope they think you're the greatest, but people who think you're the greatest and infallible are not likely to be the most honest readers. Siblings are closer to what you want, and friends and friends-of-friends who are readers and writers are closer still. Don't be afraid to ask. There's good karma in the world out there. Many people will be flattered that you ask. Get your work into other people's hands, and see what they have to say. You may be surprised in good ways and bad, but most certainly your assumptions will be both reinforced and challenged, and that's always a good thing for a writer.

At the end of the day, and (at the risk of my using two clichés in one sentence) go with your gut. Choose work that appeals to a broad audience, and at the same time, also go with the work that you truly believe in, and that you've worked hardest on.

George Saunders

Q: How should students choose their writing samples?
A: "The bell curve holds true in my experience. You've got submarine detective stories on one end, beautiful work on the other. Everything else is in the middle. You've got to push your work to the beautiful end. What I mean is, you have to not do the things that anyone else can do. Go for the stuff only you can do."

I bet you have a personal story that will shed light on this particular aspect, huh?
Oh yes. For whatever it is worth.

When I applied to the Wallace Stegner Fellowship program at Stanford University (the Stegner Program is a two year, nondegree fellowship program) I sent in two stories, "Groundskeeping" and "Bones." "Groundskeeping" was the old reliable: solid narration, description, and dialogue. "Bones" was something newer to me. It had a strong, unpredictable voice, and a changing, unpredictable narrative. "Bones" is three narratives in one, with no tangible connection among the three. My opinion at the time of my application? "Bones" was my kick-ass story, ready to change the face of the literary landscape. "Groundskeeping," on the other hand, was certainly solid, but nothing spectacular.

I also had a third story, similar to "Bones," and I thought very seriously of turning in the two newer works, and leaving "Groundskeeping" out completely.

A year later, after being accepted, I was talking about "Bones" (the newer work) with one of the committee members who was a professor at Stanford, and whose identity will be protected. He/she said: "I liked 'Bones,' but it was pretty crazy. If you'd sent two 'Bones' in, you wouldn't have made the cut. It was 'Groundskeeping' that got you in." My point? If my friend Cathy Schlund hadn't said "You should definitely send 'Groundskeeping,'" and if I hadn't said, "Really?" and if she hadn't said, "Yes, dummy," then I wouldn't have been accepted. Get your work into the hands of your readers. Listen to what they have to say. It might be a good rule of thumb to send half the work that readers admire, and half the work (half the writing sample) that you feel strongly about. Hopefully, there will be overlap between these two opinions.

I followed other people's opinions and I also followed my gut, and that balance is what you should seek when selecting your writing samples. You can't predict what one committee will like and what another committee will not like. Send your best work, and a balance of it, and let the chips fall where they may.

Bruce Snider holds an MFA in poetry and playwriting from the University of Texas Michener Center, where he later served as graduate coordinator for admissions and advising. His first book of poetry is *The Year We Studied Women*.

Q: Any tips for the writing sample?
A: "Begin strong and end strong, but particularly begin strong. Put your best work at the front of your manuscript. Readers are often more likely to forgive things later if you prove that you know what you're doing from the outset. If you're going to take some risks, and you should, do so once you've established yourself."

So, I shouldn't send new work? Or should I?
If new work means work that you wrote a week or two before the deadline, then no, you shouldn't send that in. Allowing work to sit for a while is always a good idea. Its strengths and its weaknesses will become clearer in time, and then those weaknesses can be fixed and the strengths can be expanded. Definitely send work from the last year or two of your writing experience, but don't send writing that is not yet fully formed.

Aimee Bender is a professor of English at the University of Southern California. She received an MFA in fiction from the University of California–Irvine. Her works include *The Girl in the Flammable Skirt* and *An Invisible Sign of My Own*.

Q: What advice would you offer for the writing sample?
A: "You could turn in the story you wrote years before that you received praise for, but it's wise to turn in work that you feel most connected to right now. You want to show the committee the direction you're interested in. You want to show them where you're going. You'll attract the same kind of teacher that way."

Should I send the same work to each school?

Definitely yes. Be consistent in what you choose and send. If you have stories, nonfiction, or poems A, B, C, and D, and your readers unanimously choose C and are split on A, B, and D, then definitely send C. If B is your favorite work, then send that with C, and send those two to all of your schools. Don't mix and match, hoping to get the right combination at the right school. Why not? Because if you don't get into to any schools, then you'll know that B and C are not the works to send next year. And you should be reapplying the next year if you don't get in the first time around. You want to study writing, so don't be discouraged if you aren't as successful as you'd like the first time around. Learn from the experience, and change your strategy accordingly. And whether you do get in or not, you'll have been consistent with your choices, and you won't spend the next three months (as the applications are read and as you wait to hear either way) second-guessing yourself.

If the writing sample counts 90%, then what is the next most important element?

It's kind of a tie between letters of recommendation and the personal statement. But I'll go with the letters of recommendation.

Keep in mind that the writing sample will get you into the semifinals (say, into the top thirty, from which eighteen will be chosen). These next two elements will help or hinder you into the final group.

What about the critical essay?

Good question. Again, the critical essay is likely a requirement for PhD and MA programs only. My best advice is to use your best essay sample from your undergraduate or continuing studies English work. Read it again. Edit it. Deepen it. Expand and clarify. Give it to your readers, two or more of them, and ask for feedback. Make this critical essay your very best. This element will factor in heavily for prospective PhD and MA students, right after the creative writing sample.

Who should I choose to write my letters of recommendation? What should I ask them to say? How should I go about asking them? Should I ask famous authors? What if I don't know anyone?

Whoa. All right, first things first. Keep in mind that committees expect these letters to *actually recommend* you, and to recommend you strongly. You want the letters to be good. A lukewarm recommendation can really damage your entire application. So, choose carefully the people you ask. First and foremost, choose people you can count on.

So, let's say that Emily Dickinson is still alive. If so, she'd be at least 175 years old. Let's say that you know Emily Dickinson in some capacity (or, another famous living writer instead). Would a recommendation from Ms. Dickinson help your application? Yes. Definitely. If it's a strong recommendation. A genuine endorsement from a famous and well-respected writer will definitely catch the eye of the committee.

(Yes, I know she was not famous when she was alive, smarty pants. Let's not confuse the issue here).

But which letter is better? An average letter from Emily Dickinson in which she basically says that she liked that one poem she saw of yours and that you seem like a nice person, or the letter from the community college writing instructor who has seen you in workshop and revision, and who can highly recommend your work ethic, your benefits to a workshop, and your writing talent? That isn't even a competition. It's the community college instructor hands down.

Keep that in mind as you consider whom to ask. Choose people who have insight into your ability as a student, and who will definitely recommend you. Remember that you will not see these letters, so you need to ask people you trust.

Peter Turchi directs the MFA program for writers at Warren Wilson College. His works include *Maps of the Imagination: The Writer as Cartographer*, *The Girls Next Door*, and *Magician*.

Q: What advice would you offer about letters of recommendation?

A: "Letters of recommendation can be helpful if it's evident that the recommender has some insight into the applicant's work as a student and as a writer. Letters of recommendation from friends, colleagues, agents, editors, and acquaintances are not influential. Having a "big name" recommender is not influential. . . . Applicants should choose recommenders who know them as students and/or as writers, and they should choose them carefully enough that they can allow the recommendations to be confidential. The most influential recommendations are candid: they describe the student's weaknesses as well as his or her strengths. The same is true for whatever letter of application or personal essay the student writes: one of the most helpful things for application readers to see is how the applicant perceives his or her own strengths and weaknesses. Thoughtful self-analysis is more important than a witty phrase or even publication."

Okay, who will I ask, then?

Any writing instructors from your classes are a definite on your list. But do consider other instructors you've had, in literature courses, or even not in literature courses. Remember that the graduate committee wants to know one primary thing in this letter: Is this candidate ready for graduate school and will he or she be an asset to our program? And also remember that almost all the members of the committee are teachers. Who speaks the language of teachers best? Other teachers, of course. Choose people who can comment on your academic ability and promise.

Remember that the committee will have your writing sample in front of them. They don't need letters that go on and on about your writing ability. If they don't like your poems, then a letter saying how talented you are is not going to convince them otherwise. Your letters of recommendation are intended to fill in other areas that the committee might not be aware of: academic promise, ability to work within a writing community, your reliability, and your ability to get along well with others.

It's my opinion that at least two of your three letters should come from teachers who can comment on your effectiveness in the academic and writing world. The third could come from a teacher as well, but you can also look outside that world. Perhaps someone who has supervised you in a volunteer program. Or someone who has worked with you as you organized an event. It's important that at least one of these letters, preferably more, fills in the gap between your undergraduate years and today. This person might have an insight about you that the other letter writers are not aware of.

At the end of the day, go with whom you trust, and who can comment on your promise as a student. Go with whom you've got. If you honestly don't know anyone, then it's time to start getting back into school in some way or getting involved in your local writing community.

I could really use a do's and don'ts list about letters of recommendation, preferably in bullet-point form.
The sense of entitlement in these questions is overwhelming. But, here goes:

- Do be polite about asking. No one owes you a letter.
- Do give your recommenders plenty of time to write the letters. Two months' advance time with all the supporting materials is considered common courtesy. If you don't have two months, then get in touch with them immediately.
- Do send an addressed, stamped envelope to each recommender for *each* letter. If you're applying to ten schools, the recommender will have to make nine copies of the letter. Make sure you send them ten envelopes, stamped, with the correct address on each letter.
- Do listen to me when I tell you to send a stamped envelope. Nobody likes the jerk who makes his recommenders pay for postage. They are doing you a big favor. Make the process as easy as possible for them.
- Do ask them to write their letters on their organization's letterhead if possible.

- Do send a copy of your résumé to them. They may want to comment on aspects of your experience that they need to be reminded about.
- Do send the recommendation form that the graduate program provides.
- Do ask people whom you can count on, and who will actually remember to write the letters.
- Don't send these things as you get them. Send each of your recommenders *all* of the material at once for *all* of the schools.
- Don't be afraid to ask your recommenders to comment on specific things, such as your work with revision, your participation in discussions, or your leadership abilities. Writing a recommendation can be difficult work, and if you offer your recommenders some suggestions, they'll be grateful.
- Don't hesitate to send a friendly reminder as the deadline nears.
- Don't forget to send a thank you note after they've sent the letter. Your mother will be proud, and you may need a recommendation for something else in the future. No one likes a thankless task. Make sure that writing letters on your behalf is not one of those.

Before we get into your *long* advice on personal statements, is there anything you'd like to clarify in advance?
Yes. Most programs will simply ask for a personal statement, or statement of purpose, without much direction on how to complete this. That's why I'm offering my opinion below. On the other hand, some programs will ask for specific information to be addressed. Be sure to follow the guidelines and address their questions directly.

Okay then, what can you tell me about the personal statement in general?
I guess the first thing I'd recommend about the personal statement is that you start early. Do write out a predraft of this about a month before the deadlines.

Do keep in mind that the personal statement should address your seriousness as a writer, some idea of what you'll do with your time in the graduate program, your experience related to writing, some of your interests outside of writing, a short bio, and some reasons (if possible) why you wish to attend this particular school. As

with the letters of recommendation, I don't feel like it's very important, or even helpful, to address your writing head-on. Your process
of writing—how long you've been working as a writer, how often
you write, where you hope to go with it—is definitely important.
But, including a line like "My poetry's quality and style has often
been compared to the work of Sylvia Plath" is not going to be very
helpful at all.

I also don't think it's helpful to discuss your take on the state
of twenty-first-century writing, or to include a list of writers you
admire. Perhaps your favorite poet is Mary Oliver. In my opinion, she's a great favorite to have. But a member of the committee
might not think so. Try not to tip your hand here. Certain applications will include a section for your favorite authors. Definitely
state them there. But the personal letter should stick to the issue at
hand: where you are as a person and writer right now (and where
you have been), and where you'd like to go as a person and writer by
attending this program.

**If I've done some interesting things in life, like backpacking in
Asia, or being the legal guardian of my little sister, or working
as a UPS driver, or volunteering in the Peace Corp or Teach
for America, or working as a hang-gliding instructor, should I
include these in my personal statement?**
Yes. Programs are definitely looking for well-rounded people, or
at least rounding-in-progress people. I'd traveled in Ireland extensively, where my mother was born, and I wrote a few sentences
about that in my statement. I'd also started and edited a literary
magazine in North Carolina, and I wrote briefly about that. As a
teenager, I'd worked on the NyQuil line at the Vick's (VapoRub)
factory. No joke. I included a sentence about that. Writers use their
experience in their writing. If you have some, let the committee
members know about it.

These aspects should be addressed in only a paragraph or two.
In the middle of the letter. Talk about where you have been, where
you are, but also be sure to have goals, and speak to them, about
where you are going.

How long should the letter be?
The final letter should be between one and a half pages and two
pages. No more.

How about some tips on the letter itself?

Look, before you sit down to write your letter, I think it's helpful to take stock of where you are in your writing and in your life. Though you may not use most of this information in your letter, it will be helpful in seeing yourself and your work in a clearer way. Sit down for forty minutes at your computer or notepad. Don't worry about what someone will think when they read this exercise. They're not going to. This is just for you. In fact, it may help if you write it in a "dear diary" format. So, relax and answer these questions:

1. What is the reward for writing? Why do you do it?
2. What three books have affected you the most in your life? Why, for each one?
3. What is your writing schedule (how often and where do you write)? And what would you *like* your writing schedule to be?
4. Describe the book you would like to write. Describe it on your own terms.
5. Describe your weaknesses as a writer. Describe your strengths.
6. What life events have affected your writing? What interesting things have you done (on your terms) that impact your writing?
7. What have you learned in writing classes, or other classes, that has impacted your writing?
8. How would an outside observer describe your writing?
9. When did you first start to write, and why?
10. Finally, why are you applying to these programs at this point in your life? What are you hoping to gain from this experience?

Wait a minute. Those questions address some aspects you told me *not* to address in my letter.

I know. This is not your letter. You're simply taking stock of where you are right now.

Would now be a good time to stop asking questions and to start writing?

Yes.

All right, I've written it now. It was easier than I thought, once I got going on it. Some things I wrote surprised me, in good and bad ways. What should I do now?
Set it aside for a day or two. Come back to it and reread. Think about it. Then put it away and don't look at it anymore. If you actually addressed those questions, then you know yourself better as a writer now. And that will help you write a better letter. If you didn't write this exercise, well, phooey on you.

Okay, tips on the personal letter now?
Yes.

- If you do nothing else, come across as a nice person. And a humble and curious person, at that. Be someone who others want to work with.
- The purpose of the letter is to express your writing and life background, your goals for your time in the program, and your motivation for and dedication to learning.
- Organize the document in a formal letter form. Your name and address at the top (to the right of center). The date (below, to the right of center). The name of the program and its street address (on the left). And below (and on the left) you can simply address the letter to "Selection Committee."
- Don't be afraid to state the obvious: that you're applying to this program in creative writing and you're going to explain a little about yourself and what you'd do with your time in this program.
- Introduce yourself briefly. Name, age, writing experience, academic experience, where you've lived, what you've done.
- What are you currently working on, writing wise? Don't explain it, but briefly summarize it. Summarize any relevant work you've done in the writing world (editing, workshops, publishing, etc.).
- Note: you may reference, briefly, your writing sample, but don't end up explaining it. It has to stand on its own.
- Explain what you hope to gain by attending this particular program. What will you do with the writing time? What work do you hope to complete? What classes are you interested in? Explain that you enjoy the workshop experience and have benefited from it previously. Explain that you take your

responsibilities as a student seriously. Same thing for literature classes and your other experience. Explain why you value a community of writers. (I'm assuming all these things are true.) If you're interested in teaching, explain why and what you hope to contribute and receive from the experience. Same thing about literary journals, if applicable, or community outreach.

- Always come across as a serious writer. A serious writer reads a lot and writes a lot. A serious writer, though, is not a know-it-all.
- Explain what you'd like to do, career-wise, after your graduate experience. It's just fine, and even preferable, to have your options open. But give them some idea.
- Summarize the most important points. Thank them for their consideration. Tell them that you will make the most of this experience.
- And do all these things in your own voice. My sense is that the tone should be "formal and friendly."

What if my letter turns out to be a mess?
It's probably better than you think. And in any case, it's the only one you've got. Set it aside again for a few days. Come back to it and edit it. Clarify and deepen. Make it consistent. Then, show it to two readers. Listen to their feedback, and then again, set it aside for a few days.

Finally, and this is very important: Do not edit the letter draft in the *original* computer document. Print out what you have, along with your notes for changes, and then retype the letter in a *new* document in your computer. This will help you keep the voice consistent and your points clearer.

Can I deviate from what you've recommended?
You do whatever you want. This is your letter. I feel strongest about including the personal life information and coming across as a serious writer and a nice person.

Should I reference specific professors in the program? Should I say that I've read their books and admire their work?
I'd say no. Especially if you're only referencing one or two of the professors. What if the third one reads your letter? My sense is that this will risk more harm than good.

Michael Collier is professor and codirector of the creative writing program at the University of Maryland. His works include *The Neighbor, The Folded Heart,* and, as coeditor, *The New Bread Loaf Anthology of Contemporary American Poetry.*

Q: What are some problems that committee members see in personal letters, and what advice would you offer to correct these?

A: "Often applicants don't seem to know anything about the programs they are applying to. This is because they use a generic letter. It's important that the personal statement be tailored individually to each program. This way an applicant can demonstrate the particular reason he or she is applying to that program. The personal statement should also convey something of an applicant's character and temperament, and from this can be gleaned their seriousness of purpose and sophistication as a writer."

Can I use the same letter for each program?

Sort of. You can use the bulk of the letter for each of the programs, but make each of your letters each specific in some way.

But *be sure* to change program-specific elements. This can be everything from addressing your letter to the Minnesota program as "University of Minnesota," and not the leftover from your previous letter to "Brown University" (yes, it's happened), to removing sections about teaching or working on program literary journals where that is not relevant to that program.

Get it right for each letter.

Final thoughts on the personal statement?

I guess I think of it as important. This is the only chance you have to talk about *you.* If you don't have the time necessary to write, rewrite, set aside, have others read it, set it aside again, and so on, then keep Teddy Roosevelt's mantra in mind:

Do what you can, with what you have, where you are.

Thoughts on GRE scores?

The majority of creative writing programs will require GRE scores as part of your application. How much will they count in your selection? In most cases, hardly at all.

The GRE scores are used primarily by the graduate school, as opposed to the creative writing program, for admittance to the university. The creative writing program chooses its candidates, then sends their applications on to the graduate school (basically, a department in the university) for approval. Your GRE scores need to be somewhere in the neighborhood of the scores of other graduate students at that university.

That said, you do need to take the GRE, and you should take it seriously. The GRE is offered throughout the year in computer-based format. It's not wise for me to list the procedures here. They seem to change every year.

My sense is that you need to register a month and a half ahead of time in order to find a date and location and to receive the preparation software. To receive definitive answers to these questions, go to www.gre.org.

Study for the test. Use the software and the practice tests that the GRE provides. Buy one of those GRE help books if you like. Take the practice tests, figure out where your weaknesses are, then brush up in those areas. There are definitely examples of writers who were accepted to the creative writing program but who were rejected by the graduate school. Don't be one of those people.

Do keep in mind that some universitywide fellowships are granted on the merit of undergraduate transcripts and GRE scores, so if you're applying for one of those, then yes, you should work hard to score well.

I sense that you want to clarify.

I actually want to emphasize: For the majority of schools, you do need to take the General GRE test, you do need to take it on time (so consider signing up *now*), and you need to prepare for it and do your best. But don't expect the GRE scores to be a consideration of the creative writing committee. Just remember that you can't get into the graduate school without them.

What about GRE Subject Tests?

The Literature Subject Test is mainly for prospective PhD and some MA students. Do check each program's requirements. The reading list for the Subject Test is extensive, so you'll likely need many months to prepare. Go to www.gre.org for sign-up and preparation information. I don't know of any MFA programs that require the subject test.

The Literature Subject scores will count heavily for prospective PhD and some MA students, right behind the two writing samples (creative and critical), especially for programs that lean heavily on the literature component.

What about transcripts?

Send off for your undergraduate transcripts early. Some graduate programs will want originals, not simply copies, so make sure you send off for enough of them. Allow a month's time, at least, to get this process handled. You can normally order transcripts through your undergraduate university's homepage. Some writing programs will want them sent directly to their offices, but most will allow you to include them with your application packet.

How much will your transcripts count in your application? Not as much as your letter and your recommendations, but they might count some. But why worry over it? There's not anything you can do about those grades now.

What about the application form itself?

A few programs offer online applications (where you'll actually complete the application online and *submit* it online), but the vast majority of programs will simply provide an application to download and print out. Programs that do not have at least a download-able application seem a little behind the technological curve to me. You'll have to e-mail for the application to be sent to you.

You'll get the usual in the application: name, address and so on; optional questions about your ethnicity; nonoptional questions about your residency and citizenship; a list of colleges you've attended; and so forth.

The application is normally straightforward, though there may be *two* applications: one for the creative writing program and one for the graduate school. Program websites are normally clear about this. If there is any confusion, I'd encourage you to e-mail the program coordinator.

In a few cases, the program application might ask you to indicate your favorite authors or other writing-related information. Go ahead and fill out all the information. Be clear and straightforward.

You do need to be clear and complete in your application, as an incomplete application may very well be dropped from the applicant pool before anyone even sees your writing sample. In most cases, the application itself will not be heavily considered in the selection process. But, obviously, you won't be considered as a candidate if you haven't completed it in full.

Other items in the application?

The application fee. Don't forget that, by check or money order. By the way, most of these will range from $40 to 55 dollars. I suppose I'd pay $60 or, reluctantly, $65. Anything more than that and I'd seriously reconsider the program. An application fee should cover the cost of processing and the committee work. It shouldn't be a profit-making venture for the program.

It's also a good idea to include a self-addressed, stamped postcard with your application, whether the program asks for one or not. When you include a postcard, the program will mail it back to you so you'll know your application arrived in full.

Some programs may have a more complicated application, with shorter essays in a variety of areas. Other programs may ask for a teaching philosophy statement. I know of one program that asks for a self-critique of an applicant's writing. Obviously, if a program asks for something in addition to the items I've listed, be sure to send it.

What if I have something else that they haven't asked for? Can I send that?

Few programs ask for a résumé or a cv (curriculum vitae). I think it's okay to send one if you feel like it. However, it should not stand in replacement of your personal statement. If a program is not interested in the résumé, they'll just toss it and keep what they need. That said, a résumé in this case should last only two pages.

I'm not saying you should send a résumé. I'm saying I think it is okay if you can't control yourself.

I hope this is obvious: I would recommend against sending newspaper clippings about yourself or a homemade video or the like. You'll seem amateurish and immature, whether that's the case or not. Stick to the items you've been asked for, and address other items in your personal statement.

Final Thoughts?

Remember that your writing sample is, by far, the most important element of your application. In that sense, this is a very different application than your undergraduate application or applications for other graduate degrees. By your senior year in high school, you knew what your grades were and you knew what your SAT scores were. Consequently, you had a general idea of which colleges you would get into, and which you would not. It's similar for, say, law school graduate students when they factor in their undergraduate transcripts and their LSAT scores.

But for the graduate degree in creative writing, it's the writing sample, and almost the writing sample only. 90 percent of how you'll be judged will be based on your writing. This element makes the "prediction" process very difficult. You don't really know where you stand a good chance and where you don't. So, it behooves you to send them in your work and find out. And it also behooves you to apply to a number of schools (eight to twelve), and finally, you are behooved to control what you can control—your application and its contents, your criteria for selecting schools—and to not worry too much about the rest.

Chapter Summary

1.   Your application materials for most creative writing programs will include: Your writing samples, three letters of recommendation, a personal statement, undergraduate (and other, if applicable) transcripts, GRE scores, the application form, and the application fee.

1A. Applications to PhD programs and some MA programs will require GRE Literature Subject scores and a critical essay.

2.   Apply to eight to twelve programs. Keep your options open.

3.   The writing sample is, by far, the most important element in your application. Be sure to give your work to readers and writers and listen to their comments about the strength of the work.

4. For your letters of recommendation, choose people whom you trust and who can comment effectively on your academic achievements and potential.

5. The personal statement should address who you are, what you have done in your life, why you're ready for graduate work, and what you will do with your time in the program. Don't spend too much time addressing your writing directly. Do address your writing-related *experience*, but know that your writing sample must speak for itself.

6. The GRE and college transcripts are necessary parts of the application process in most cases. They don't count heavily, but you can't be accepted without them.

7. The application process can be complicated. Make a schedule and stick to it.

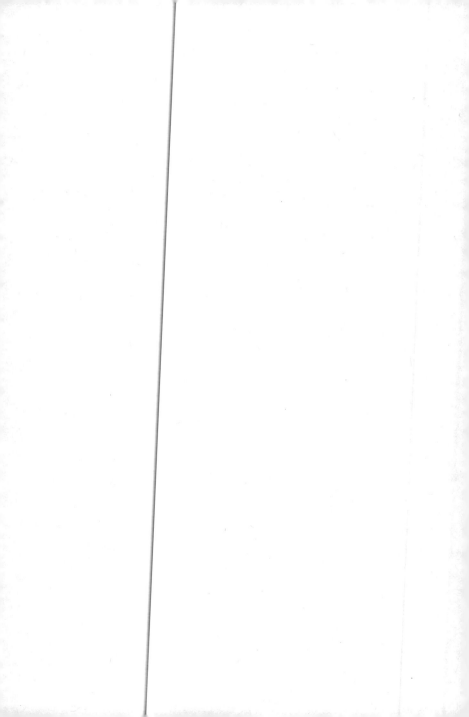

Checklist for Applying to Creative Writing Programs

_____ Read this book so you know what you're getting in to.

_____ Decide on what criteria you'll use in selecting your programs. What tops your list? Funding, location, teaching experience, faculty? Make a list of must haves and a list of like-to-haves.

_____ Narrow your search to about thirty programs. They are listed by state at the back of this book, and there is also the profile of fifty in chapter three. Yes, by all means, include some of the "top" programs, but also include smaller, lesser-known programs. Spread your net wide and keep your chances for acceptance high.

_____ Read over the websites of these programs. Yes, all of them. Break them into groups of five and read them over the course of one or two weeks. While you're moving along, keep a list of definitely apply, likely apply, and maybe apply.

_____ If you know someone who has attended a creative writing graduate program, by all means do talk with them. They may have insights not only into their own program, but into other programs as well. And, about programs in general. If it's a friend of a friend of a friend, don't hesitate to contact him or her. People enjoy talking about their experiences. You may pick up some tips or insights.

_____   If you are confused about anything involving a program,
          contact the program coordinators/administrators by
          e-mail. That's what they're there for. Do try and keep
          your questions limited to one e-mail. No one likes a
          noodge. And be sure to be polite. While program
          coordinators likely won't have a say in the acceptance
          process, they do work in the same offices as people who
          do. If you seem like a pain in the neck, then that word
          will get around.

_____   When you have the information you need, sit down and
          make your decisions about the twelve or so programs
          that you'll apply to. Include a mix of "top" programs
          and lesser-known programs. Be sure to talk this out
          with someone: a roommate, a sibling, a friend, even if
          they have no experience in creative writing. Sometimes
          you simply need a sounding board to get your decisions
          organized. When you've made your final decision on the
          twelve, be at peace with it. You've done your research.
          You've used good criteria. Be happy about your choices,
          and don't second-guess yourself.

_____   Download or request materials from schools, including
          the forms for recommenders. Make an 'organized' chart
          similar to the one in chapter 4.

_____   Decide who you'll need letters of recommendation
          from. Try to do this two months ahead of the deadline.
          Contact these people as soon as possible. You'll need
          three, so consider three and two backups. Contact the
          first three. Be clear about deadlines, and be sure, once
          they have said yes, to send them all of the materials
          they'll need in one package. Be polite and grateful. No
          one owes you a letter. Do send clear instructions with
          your packet. Some letters will go directly to programs,
          others will be sent to you in sealed envelopes. Include
          stamped, addressed envelopes in your packet, for the
          convenience of the recommenders.

_____   Send off for transcripts from your undergraduate or
          continuing studies institutions. Allow two to three

weeks for the transcripts to arrive. Be aware that most programs will ask you to simply include the transcripts with your application, though others will ask that the transcripts be sent directly to their office.

_____ Go to the GRE website. Sign up for the appropriate tests, either General or General and Literature. Give yourself a few weeks to study and prepare yourself. Give yourself more time if you're taking the GRE Literature Test. Buy one of those GRE books or use the preparation material that the GRE provides, take the practice tests, and then work on areas necessary for improvement.

_____ Think about your writing sample. If you have four stories you're thinking about sending (you'll send only two), then give copies to readers you trust and who will give you an honest opinion. Give them to three or four people. Same thing if you have eighteen poems and will send only nine. Listen to what people have to say. Then, sleep on it for a week. At the end of the process, go with your gut. Send the work that you believe is of the highest quality.

_____ Complete the writing exercise I've included in chapter 4. Think about where you are in your writing and in your life. This will be good preparation for your personal statement, and for your program experience.

_____ Take the GRE. My mom would say, "Get a good night's sleep beforehand, and eat a good breakfast." That's good advice. Thanks, Mom. Have your scores sent to your schools.

_____ Be sure to polish your writing samples. Edit them and make them better. I don't recommend writing something brand new. By that, I mean an entire new story or poem. You may certainly add new sections to existing works. Go with your polished, complete work. Have someone read for copyediting and for consistency. Don't let a typo distract program readers from the quality of your work.

_____ Write your personal statement. Be sure to address the areas I mentioned in the previous chapter and, of course, the directions of the program. Be friendly and formal. Make sure you come across as a serious writer and a nice person. Set the statement aside for a day or two. Edit it. Give it to two readers. Listen to their comments. Make your final changes. Your final letter should be a page and a half to two pages.

_____ Fill out copies of the applications in pencil. Figure out any problem areas you need to contend with.

_____ Fill out the applications in pen, or online.

_____ If you haven't heard back from your recommenders with two weeks to go before the deadlines, send a friendly reminder.

_____ Get everything together. Go back to your chart. Lay all the necessary materials out on the floor, in piles for each school. Double-check the contents. Then, send them off a week before the deadlines. Sooner, if you want. If you're down to the wire, be aware that some schools require delivery by the deadline, and others require postmarks by the deadline. Use overnight delivery if you're pushing things.

_____ Take a deep breath. Go out to dinner with a friend. Celebrate a little. That was harder than you thought it'd be, but you got it done on time. Now, get back to your life, and allow your application to do its work. You'll hear back in early April, and there's nothing further for you to do till then.

_____ Nice job.

CHAPTER 5

Decision Time

> Tracy K. Smith is a professor of English at the University of Pittsburgh. She received her MFA from Columbia University and was later a Wallace Stegner Fellow at Stanford University. *The Body's Question* is her first book of poetry.
>
> Q: How does one make a final decision about the programs?
> A: "I think one of the main things you can go on is a gut feeling, but only if you know what you're dealing with. Visit each of the programs. Sit in on a workshop. Get a sense of the workshop, and of the program. What will the community be like? Get a sense of the spirit governing the place. Students and faculty may change, but for the most part the environment will not. This will help you eliminate some programs from your list, and it will move you toward others."

Okay, you've sent your applications, you've returned to your normal life, and now you're waiting to hear. You'll start receiving responses in late March to early April. Decision time will come next. You'll likely need to choose from your options by mid- to late April, and in general, you'll only have about two weeks to make your decision. Make sure you're prepared for those weeks.

I've applied to eight to twelve programs. How many will I be accepted to?

You've applied to that many programs so you'd have some options. It would be best if you were accepted to three or more, but even two will offer some options for your final decision. You won't be accepted everywhere simply because different schools and committee members have different tastes. For the purpose of most of this chapter, let's assume you've been accepted to three programs.

What if I'm not accepted anywhere?

That's certainly a possibility. First of all, don't take it personally. You sent your work, you let the chips fall where they may, and they didn't happen to fall your way this time. I know of many current and former creative writing graduate students who were not accepted on their first try. So don't give up. Read a lot, write a lot. Receive feedback on your writing. My best advice is: shake your reading list up. Seek new work, read new work. Take a writing class. Apply again the next year, to a mix of schools: half where you've previously applied, half new schools. Send new work. Rejection is part of being a writer, and so is perseverance. If you're serious about writing, then you can make this happen. Keep your chin up, and apply again in the fall.

You said that the criteria for my final decision will be different from the "application" criteria. What should I be looking at now?

Funding moves up to a definite number one. If one program offers funding far and above your other acceptances, then I'd go with that one. A program that funds its students will support its students in other ways as well. If funding is similar, or if tuition is about the same, then move on to the other criteria.

Keep in mind that health care is part of funding, and we all know that health care is expensive. Make sure you know what kind of health plans are offered by the university, and factor this into your funding decision.

Location moves down to number two. You've already narrowed your original search to places where you want to live and places where you can stand to live. Now, if you've always wanted to live in New York City, or in rural Indiana, or on the coast of Florida, or in the deserts of Arizona, go for it. Making a life for yourself in your new home is every bit as important as what you'll learn inside the program.

Teaching stays at number three, at least for most people. Most people will want teaching experience, but not *too much* teaching experience. Any program that makes you teach more than one class a semester is a program I'd be wary of. A program that offers teaching experience some semesters, and writing, research, or editing fellowships for some other semesters is a good choice. You'll want experience, and you may also want a break from that experience. I taught every semester when I was at UMass, and I actually liked that and benefited from it. So, one class a semester is about right. Above that is problematic, below that (but not none, obviously, if you want the experience) is better. Take stock of what classes you'll be teaching. You won't want to teach composition for three years. Keep your eye on programs that offer experience teaching creative writing and other classes at some point during your career.

Faculty stays at number four, but there is more emphasis now. Read the work of professors in the program. You're not necessarily looking for similarities in your writing, though that may be a good thing. You're looking for writing that is interesting to you, and from which you might learn more about.

You left something out, didn't you?

It's not that I left something out, it's that I want to emphasize something in particular: Make sure, once you are accepted to a program, that you ask for contact numbers and e-mail addresses of current students. Call them up, talk with them, ask them about the program, campus, location, teaching experience, professors, and general atmosphere. I'd recommend that you speak with at least three students at each school. Getting a "feel" for the program from its current students will guide you in great measure in your decision. Keep the main criteria in mind, but seek insight into the program from those who know best.

For the most part, current students are very happy to talk to newly admitted students. Make sure you have a list of a half dozen questions before you call.

George Saunders

Q: What's the best way to research programs, especially the faculty?

A: "Always ask current students. I can't emphasize that enough. One of the unknowns about faculty is, are they there? If William Shakespeare is on faculty, is he teaching most semesters, or does he teach one class every four years? It happens. Are they there for real, or are they just there on paper? Ask the current students. Students on the ground will know what it's like on the ground. E-mail is a great way to do this. A good program will facilitate you in contacting current students. . . . Ask about the program director. The atmosphere of the program comes from the top down. If someone runs the program like a fiefdom, then that's something you want to stay away from. It happens. On the other hand, if someone shows affection for students, is interested in their work and in their lives, works to make them feel important and valued, actively promotes the community, then that's what you want."

Did you ask your interviewees for questions I should ask current students?

Of course I did. I'm always thinking.

Thanks to Rachel Kadish, Padma Viswanathan, Maria Hummel, Scott McCabe, and Aimee Bender for this list.

Obviously, you'll pick and choose as you see fit. Be a good interviewer, not an inquisitor, and you'll get the best answers.

- Regarding the city or town: Is the money you are given sufficient to live on? Is it isolated or urban? Is it safe or dangerous? Is the university integrated into the rest of the community? What are the rents in places where students live?
- How expensive is it to live there? How do students make it?
- Is the program director and faculty responsive to student concerns? How much time and attention do you get from the faculty? What do you think of the professors as teachers of writing (as opposed to what you think of them as writers)?

- "I'd ask them how their writing is going. If I talk with three students, and they're all having trouble writing, then that's probably not a program I want to attend. That sounds obvious, but it's important."
- Does the workshop have a preferable style, and if you don't write that way, are you out of luck? Can different styles coexist in the workshop?
- How much of a say do students have in planning their own curriculum? To what degree are the students active agents in their personal and creative direction?
- "I'd want a general sense of the workload. A specific sense is even better. What is the workload? What is your life like as a student?"
- Do you think the progress you've made warrants your enrolling in the program? Have you seen substantial progress in your work that could not have been made on your own?
- What is the community within the program like?
- What do other graduates go on to do? Do they settle in that area? Do they publish? Do they get fellowships elsewhere? Do you receive some kind of counseling about how to move into the writing world after the program?
- What do you wish you'd known going in? What surprised you about the program?
- "I'd ask how has their writing changed. I want to know if the program encourages students to pay attention to that."

What if I'm accepted to a program or programs, but I'm not offered any funding?

Then that's a decision you'll have to make. You'll want to see if the tuition and other expenses are affordable to your situation. I would encourage you to talk to the administrator, or better yet, the program director at each of the schools. Tell them about your financial situation. There may be other funding options, or there may be a waiting list for funding (in case other students do not accept offers, which happens often). Keep your options open.

Some program directors may hold out hope of funding in the second year of the program. Take those comments with a grain of salt. In these cases, I'd bet your chances for future funding are about fifty–fifty. If you're willing to take that risk, go for it.

And if you're not offered funding but are determined to attend a program nonetheless, I'd encourage you to do so. Many programs, especially state universities, are affordable. Seek residency in the program's state, as this will reduce tuition greatly. Seek out jobs on campus, as these sometimes come with a tuition waiver. Apply to grants and fellowships that are offered by the university and by outside organizations. Work hard over the summer. Save your money.

I emphasize funding because I believe a writer should learn to live cheaply, at least early in his or her career, and because a program that funds its students is a program that supports its students. So, keep those things in mind. But also keep in mind: there are a number of hurdles to overcome in your writing career, and funding at your program may be one of those. If you're determined to improve your craft, to set aside time for your writing, and to become part of a writing community, then by all means, make the financial investment in yourself. The one thing I would add is: ask the program coordinator about current students who are paying full tuition. Get in touch with them by phone. Ask them about the program in general, but at some point ask about how the nonfunded students are treated there. Many programs with fewer financial resources still offer other types of resources. If those current students are happy with their situation, then you likely will be, too.

What if I'm "wait-listed" for a program?

This is just what it sounds like. As an example, twelve students have been accepted for twelve slots at program C. But the program director knows that not all the students will accept the offer. So, there's a waiting list of a half dozen students. If you're on it, feel free to ask what number you are. They may tell you, they may not.

If you're number one on the list you'll likely be accepted, but I said "likely," not definitely. You should feel free to talk to the program coordinator or director about your chances. Don't be pushy, but ask directly and clearly. Make a good impression, as the phone call or e-mail might actually help your chances a lot.

Some schools don't have waiting lists at all. They'll look to gain twelve students by accepting eighteen. And yes, they'll take all eighteen if every student accepts, but that is rare.

What if I have to make a decision at programs A and B, but I haven't yet heard from program C?

You should have heard something by April 15. Most programs will ask you to decide by mid- to late April. If program A is pressing you for an answer, don't hesitate to call program C and let them know that. Your tone should be "I've been offered acceptance at one (or more) other programs, and I wanted to know when I might hear from your program. I've got to make a decision by the end of this week," and less of "What's the holdup? Don't you know I've got to make a very important decision here?"

By all means, get in contact. Phone is fine, e-mail is fine.

Remember that I said *If program A is pressing you.* Don't get on the phone with the other programs the minute you've been accepted to your first school. Keep a level head, and see what comes your way.

Can I "bargain" or "negotiate" with programs about funding?

To a certain extent. Do keep in mind: if a program funds all its students equally, or if there is no funding at all, then there is nothing to negotiate.

Yet let's say that program A offers great funding, but is located in a place you're not that excited about. And let's say that program B offers average funding, but is located in your favorite city and has an author on faculty that you're really excited about. There's nothing wrong with contacting program B and telling them the situation. They may very well up the ante. My funding was in doubt at UMass, and when I called to talk about it, I receive a "We'll see what we can do." As it turned out, they did a lot, and I had a teaching position two days later.

I doubt if a program director can give you an answer on the spot. But there's nothing wrong with making your needs and preferences clear and asking if there is some leeway with funding. Show your enthusiasm for that particular program, and, again, see what comes your way.

Padma Viswanathan is a student in the MFA fiction program at the University of Arizona. She holds an MA in creative writing from the Johns Hopkins University.

Q: Can students bargain with programs?
A: "I never thought of it as bargaining. I stated my needs and asked what options I had. At one time I had an offer from two schools. The first school's offer was not nearly as good as the second. I was very honest with them about it. They came back to me with another offer, which was much more substantial, though it still didn't quite match up. But then the second school increased their offer too, without my having said anything to them. I was just hesitating and thinking things over. I ended up taking the best offer. . . . Almost all my correspondence was by e-mail. I chose this because I wanted to word it exactly. I didn't wish to alienate anyone. It's important to remember that all of these people are potential future colleagues. The advice I would offer students is to be honest and negotiate in good faith. You're not playing them off one another. You're simply seeking the best situation for yourself. Put it in writing so that you're saying exactly what you want. No more, no less. . . . It was interesting that one program, that I did not attend, asked me to write a letter, explaining that funding was a major factor in my decision. They wanted to use my decision in negotiations with the administration, to show they were losing students because of a lack of resources."

Should I really be contacting/calling/e-mailing the programs this much?

I never said to contact the programs/directors/coordinators/current students all the time. Don't become an annoyance. Get your questions in mind and make the most of each contact.

Will programs offer an "admit weekend," where I can visit the program?

Not many will, but some do. I think very highly of these programs, and so should you. It shows that they are actively recruiting their graduate students, and that they have the resources and initiative to do so. Definitely attend the weekend, and see what you can find out.

Can I defer my acceptance for a year?

In some cases. I'd say about a third of schools will allow you to do this if you have a good reason. But if you don't have a good reason, why hesitate? Go.

Hey, this is a big decision here. This is my life we're talking about here. Why is this the last question in this very short chapter?

You're right, this is a big decision, and I'm not about to make it for you. When you're accepted to a program, visit its website again. Refresh your memory about its strengths and weaknesses. Talk to the program coordinator and director. Definitely, definitely, definitely talk with current and former students. Ask questions about whatever is most important to you: classes, program atmosphere, the feel of the town or city, health care, readings, publications, and other opportunities.

If you have the resources to visit the programs, do so. Check them out firsthand.

Make a list of the pros and cons of each program. Sit down and talk them out with someone. A good friend, writer or not. Someone who is a good listener and who will tell you what they "hear" from you. Explain your criteria and how each program measures up, or not. Talk about what you want to experience in the next two or more years, and how each program might fulfill your needs. Don't allow the person to make the decision for you, but instead ask him or her to repeat back what is heard from you. A friend's best role is to help you organize your thoughts and to reflect back your own opinions.

Lean toward funding heavily, but keep your other criteria in mind. Make your decision. Sleep on it. If you feel good about it in the morning, you'll feel good about it for the years to come.

Congratulation on your acceptance(s). Make your decision. And make it your own.

Chapter Summary

1. Acceptances and rejections will start arriving in late March and early April. You'll need to make a final decision on your program by mid- to late April.

2. Criteria to use in your final decision: Funding is a definite one, and health care is part of funding. Location stays at number two. Teaching experience is three, whether you want teaching experience or you *don't* want teaching experience. Either way, stay away from programs that offer *too much* teaching (more than one class a semester). Faculty stays at four, but is more important for this final decision. Read the work of your potential professors and see what you think.

3. The most important action you can take is to talk with current and former students about their experience in the program. Talk with at least three students from each program to get an accurate read on the atmosphere and resources of the program.

4. If you are not accepted to any programs, don't take it personally. Many current and past creative writing graduate students were not accepted on their first application. Read a lot, write a lot over the next few months. Shake up your reading list. Create new work, and apply again. Include new schools in the fall.

5. If funding is not offered at any of your accepted programs, then talk to the program directors there about other sources of financial support. Talk with current students about how less-funded students are treated in the program. Make your decision based on these conversations and of course your current financial situation.

6. Do contact programs if you haven't heard from them by April 15. Be clear about when you have to make your decisions about other programs. Do this also for any schools that have you wait-listed. Be polite.

7. I'm not sure if "bargain" is the right word, but you can make your offers from programs clear to the directors of other programs. Do ask if they can match that offer. There's no harm in asking, and sometimes there is great help in it.

8. Talk out the pros and cons of each program with a friend. Ask that person to repeat back what he or she has heard. Use your criteria, and lean heavily on funding. Make your decision, sleep on it, and see if you feel right about it in the morning. Make your decision your own.

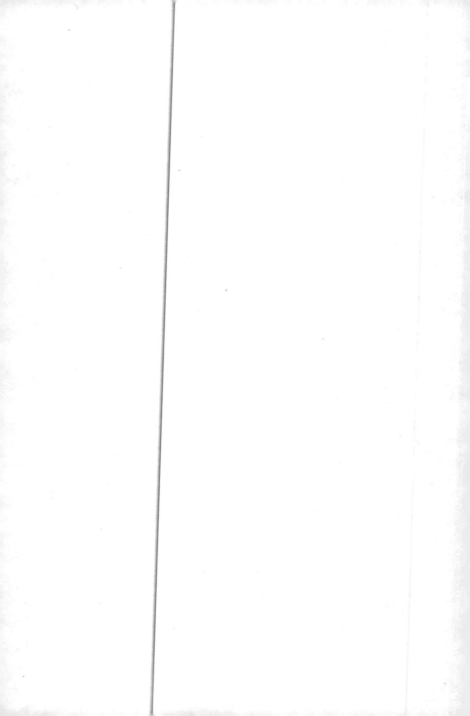

CHAPTER 6

Your Graduate Program

Geoffrey Wolff

Q: Do you have any advice for students entering a program?

A: "Students are naturally shocked at the amount of work they enlisted for. They take a course about teaching, they teach, they prepare work for workshop, they study and comment on their colleagues' work. Then they endure what Camus termed the "fleas of life": where to live, how to furnish it, where a car can be repaired, who's a good dentist, where do you go to have a good time. It can be overwhelming. That's why it's crucial stray awake during the summer before the program starts. Write up a storm that summer. Arrive with new work. That's the most profitable advice I can offer: Hit the ground running, and you'll be happy."

All right, you've arrived. Or are about to. Having a plan, or at least some goals, when you arrive is a key. What are those goals and plans? That's not really any of my business. My goals when I arrived at the University of Massachusetts were to complete a book, improve my writing, make some friends, learn to teach, live a variety of experiences, keep my sanity and health, and keep in touch with my friends and family. For the most part, I accomplished all of these things.

So, read this chapter over. I hope to provide some insights on what you can expect in your program. Afterward, take a few minutes and write down some goals for yourself, as well as some plans for getting these accomplished. By all means, stay loose, stay flexible, but keep one eye on the goals you've set out for yourself.

Should I visit the program and city/town before my program starts?

Definitely yes. I'd suggest traveling there a month ahead of time. Why? Because this will facilitate finding a necessity: housing. (More soon.) You'll also meet the program coordinator, perhaps a professor (keep in mind that they are often away for the summer), and get to know the campus. Take a campus tour. Get in contact with a few second- and third-year students. E-mail them directly once you get contact information from the coordinator. And when I say e-mail them directly, I don't mean sending out a mass e-mail. I mean writing three or four students directly to say hi and to ask if you can talk with them about the program over the summer. Then, get back in contact with them before you arrive. See if you can meet up with them for coffee. Maybe they'll offer to show you around town or introduce you to other students.

If someone offers to put you up for a night, take them up on the offer. Otherwise, check in to a local hotel. A three- or four-day stay sounds about right.

What about housing?

The program coordinator should have some advice on this. But the best advice will come from current students. Some former students may be leaving, and you might check out their former residences. Check the classifieds online before you go. Set up appointments with landlords. It is *very* important to get suggestions on parts of town, or towns outside of the town, from current students before you go. Don't be afraid to ask. Many programs include a "survival guide," written by students, on their websites. Study this thoroughly.

My best advice? Visit five or six apartments. If at all possible, sign no more than a six-month lease, unless you're really in love with a place. Keep your options open. You may find another neighborhood, or a roommate situation you like better.

Arrive with your checkbook, and the phone numbers and addresses of previous landlords. If you don't have these things, you're sunk. So be sure to pack them.

Will you live with roommates or get a place by yourself? Depending on your financial situation, and your relationship situation, and the cost of living in that area, this question may have one or more answers. Do think about it ahead of time. Explore both options if you're not sure. Explore the option of living with current students, but definitely explore the option of roommates outside of the program. Having a life outside the program—especially after the first half year—can be important to your sanity.

I guess my best advice is to visit the location, tour around, visit as many rooms/apartments as you can, then sign a short-term lease.

If it's not possible for you to visit ahead of time, then do what you can in the first few days that you arrive, using this same advice.

If I'm moving to another state, should I become a resident?
Definitely yes. As soon as possible. On a very basic level, you'll be aided by having in-state tuition, which will be helpful if you're paying for your education, or if your funding level is subject to change. On a more complex level, your residency will aid you in aspects from driver's licenses, voting, and eligibility for everything from library cards to grants and fellowships.

Go to the new state's main website and find the information about becoming a resident. Some states will make this easy, others difficult. Either way, get it done.

What sort of class load should I take?
I'd recommend taking a high number of classes right from the beginning. By high I mean three or four. Why? First, it will immerse you in the program. You'll meet many more of your fellow students that way, as well as many of the professors. Second, you'll either be ahead or you'll be on schedule to finish your classes by the end of your stay. You'll appreciate extra time later, especially as you begin to think and work on your thesis.

Which classes should I take?
A workshop will likely be required each semester of the first year. There may be some specific required first-year classes. Obviously,

take those. Otherwise, a contemporary fiction, poetry, or nonfiction class is always a good bet. Go ahead and concentrate on the required courses for your first semester and year. Save your electives and other flexible classes for when you're clearer about your interests and needs.

As always, ask veteran students about the best teachers and classes.

Maria Hummel

Q: Any classes that were particularly helpful to you?
A: "One class that was very practical was Editing and Publishing. I learned all the typographical marks. We wrote papers about the publishing world. I did one paper on the gutting of the midlist in children's fiction and one on poetry contests. The class made me consider the publishing world as an industry, and, depressing as it was, that helped me to be realistic and informed in my goals. Later, I also ended up working as an editor to support myself, so the course was very useful to me."

What can you tell me about teaching, and about workshop?
I've included longer sections on these in chapters 6A and 6B.

What about the social aspect of a graduate program?
What to say, what to say. . . . First off, you'll likely notice that there are stark similarities between the first year of graduate school and the first year of undergraduate school. By that I mean you're suddenly placed in a new situation, meeting lots of people, learning new ideas, reading new work, socializing in different places, and becoming a new person. To some extent or another. For lack of a better term, there's a kind of giddiness to the first year of graduate school. People stay out late, they make new friends, maybe an enemy or two, they gossip about others, they fail at things, succeed at others. By all means, enjoy all this. But keep grounded in some way. I think it's a very good idea to create an outlet *outside* of the graduate program. That may be a weekend job at a restaurant; a yoga, dance, or drawing class; joining a gym; hanging out with

nonwriter neighbors; or joining a running or rock-climbing club. Whatever seems best to you. Keeping an aspect of your life outside of the program will pay huge dividends: you'll have a place to decompress from the pressures and thrills of graduate school, and you'll be able to keep your graduate experience in perspective, and therefore you'll be able to enjoy it to a greater extent.

As far as the graduate program goes, there will be readings, seminars, on-campus events, and program parties. Informally, workshop members may meet at a bar or coffee shop after class, there will certainly be graduate student parties, some students may form reading or studying groups, and there will be weekend outings and road trips. Make friends, meet new people, make time for these events. Enjoy yourself. These may be some of the best years of your life. (Music swells, light dims, sun sets in the distance. . . .) But keep an outlet, so you can keep it in perspective.

And don't forget the life you had before graduate school. Make time for family and friends, either by visits or by phone and e-mail. Do go home or travel during your winter and spring breaks and some longer weekends. Don't lose sight of where you've come from, even if you're headed somewhere else.

Maria Hummel

Q: Any advice on the social aspects of a program?
A: "Do get to know your classmates. Some of my favorite memories of the program were ad-hoc dinners with my friends Michele, Jenn, and David. We'd pass around books. We'd say, 'Have you read this? Isn't this great?' I learned as much from those nights as I did from workshop. It was an extension of the classroom, but with cheap red wine. . . . We're sometimes isolated as writers, and when you get to an MFA program it may be the first time in your life that you're surrounded by creative freaks like yourself. It's exhilarating. That said, don't let it take over. You have a lot of time, and that's good, but you can't party with your friends every moment. Most of us only get that two years. Make sure you're using that time for writing."

I've got a partner/girlfriend/boyfriend who I'm going to do "long-distance" with. Any tips?

Well, my best advice is to go ahead and break up now, and save both of you a lot of trouble.

Funny, funny, ha, ha. But, I'm only being half-funny. Or trying to. You're going to immerse yourself in a lot of new experiences, and you're going to meet a lot of new people. Consequently, your long-distance relationship is going to feel a lot of strain. What I can tell you is this: when a partner/girlfriend/boyfriend moves with the graduate student, then all will likely be well. When the couple has a plan to be together within a year, all has a good chance to be well. When the couple has ambiguous plans to eventually be together at some unspecified time in the future, they're sunk.

So, if you value your relationship, either move together to the new town, or make plans to be together in the very near future (no longer than a year). Any lack of a plan will likely result in a lack of a relationship.

What's your best overall advice for making the most of my first year?

I've said this before, and I'll say it again in the teaching chapter: Make sure you speak with and learn from veteran students. Meet with them, buy them a cup of coffee, ask questions, listen. They have all sorts of insights that will help you avoid pitfalls and help you make the most of your graduate experience.

What about writing? Isn't that what I'm here to do?

It sure is.

- Set aside a place for your writing. That may be a separate office in your apartment if you have room. It may be a desk moved into a corner. It may be a favorite table at a coffeehouse or library. Set aside a place where you will write, and write only. That place will be for your creative work, not for checking e-mail, surfing the Web, answering the phone, grading papers, reading for class, or any other distraction. Save a place for writing, and your writing will prosper.
- Set aside time for writing. Set a schedule, and stick to it. This may vary from writer to writer, but I'd suggest four or five

blocks of time each week, two to four hours, where you will work with your writing. Write out the schedule and post it somewhere. Keep it a priority.

- Write every day. Four hours would be great. But on your busier days, even simple outlines/notes/scenes/stanzas in your notebook for fifteen minutes can help a lot. Keep in practice with your writing, and it will take less time to get warmed up when you actually have large blocks of time in your writing schedule.

- Work on a few projects at once. I'm not talking a dozen. I'm talking three or four. They may be in different stages: first draft, editing, final draft, fun. When you get bored with one, or if you're blocked with another, you'll always have something to work on. Sometimes it helps one work when you ignore it consciously to work on another. Often, your unconscious mind is still working on the other.

- How can you deal with writer's block? Balance your time. You are outputting onto the page, so make sure you input in your life. Be *with* people. Get out and go for a walk. Do things at night or in the morning that are not writing-related. Travel. Indulge another artistic expression such as drawing, photography, or music. Don't allow these to infringe on your writing schedule, but do schedule them, even for short amounts of time in the rest of your life schedule.

- The best cure for writer's block is reading. Read a lot, write a lot, and at appropriate times receive feedback on your writing. If you've been staring at the computer screen for too long, pick up a book and dive in to it for a half hour. Often, seeing words on the page will jump-start your own words. I think people often worry too much about being overly influenced by work dissimilar to their own. Dissimilar work can actually be a big help. You can see what you want to do that is different, or you can learn techniques and craft that is applicable to your work. If you can't write, then read. And then write.

- Don't be discouraged by what you read. By that I mean, if you read your favorite writer and then despair about your own level of craft, that's not helping you. The solution is *not* to stop reading great work. The solution is to allow yourself a draft. Get words on paper, then see what to do about them.

Do what you can with what you have, where you are. I'm not saying that you are a novice at the craft, but I am saying that all writers were novices at some point. We are all working to improve. Allow yourself that goal of improvement. It comes in stages, not in leaps and bounds. Be steady and consistent, and you'll make your progress.

- If you're really stuck, then getting an outside opinion can be of great help. Give your work to friends, or fellow students. Listen to what they have to say. You may simply need a nudge in a direction or two to jump-start your creative mind.

What can you tell me about public readings?
Go to them. Especially when your fellow students are giving them or when the program has brought in an outside writer. Or, obviously, when one of your professors is reading. You'll support your colleagues and program. And, you'll likely hear great or at least interesting work, and you'll have the chance to socialize afterward.

How should I interact with my professors?
Get to know them. This can be informally, after class or after readings, or formally, during class or in office hours. The vast majority of creative writing professors care about their students and their students' careers. Read the work of your professors, and be familiar with it. Ask for advice about your creative work, your career options, a reading list. Speak to veteran students about which professors are helpful and insightful.

> **Victoria Chang holds an MFA from Warren Wilson College, and she is currently a PhD candidate at the University of Southern California. Her first book of poetry is *Circle*.**
>
> **Q:** What's the workload for a low-residency program?
> **A:** "They'll tell you that it's twenty to twenty-five hours a week, and that's pretty accurate. It's good practice for living the life of a writer. It teaches you good habits. I spend twenty to twenty-five hours a week on my writing now, and that's because of the program. You get what you put into it. It's difficult, but you get used to it, and if you're serious about it, you look forward to that time."

It seems like a lot of these answers have to do with residency programs, as opposed to low-residency programs.
I think so too. That's why there's a great interview with Scott McCabe, a graduate of the Lesley University low-residency program in chapter 6A. Check it out.

What can you tell me about publishing and literary magazines?
See chapter 6B.

How do I get a literary agent?
I knew this was coming. First of all, this is likely for fiction and nonfiction writers, primarily. Poets often enter their manuscripts in book contests, as do many short story writers. There are links to contest information in appendix B.

In any case, here are my thoughts on agents.

Before you look for an agent, you should have built up a résumé of magazine publications. Somewhere around half a dozen sounds right. You'll likely be looking for an agent after your graduate experience, when you've completed a book to your satisfaction. Your graduate experience is about learning your craft and concentrating on reading and writing.

Some people find agents through referrals. People who might refer you are friends, professors, or fellow students. Keep in mind: a referral is a big thing. No one is going to refer you to his or her agent if he or she is not enthusiastic about your work. Make certain that is the case before you ask. Otherwise, you're likely to be turned down, and you'll likely turn that person off.

The main thing you need to do is buy the *Guide to Literary Agents* by Writers Digest Books. Read it thoroughly, especially the advice sections. Pay close attention to advice on query letters, as this is how you start the process of contacting an agent. There are listings of hundreds of agents and agencies in the book. Do think about the writers who you admire and who write in similar ways to you. Research their agents, in the book and on the Web.

One of the most important aspects in finding and selecting an agent is the query letter. In the letter, list your experience and publications, state why you are interested in this particular agency, and explain in a couple paragraphs about the work you are seeking to sell. Yes, you sometimes hear about writers who sell a novel or other book based on a first chapter or simply a proposal. But for the most part, publishers (and therefore agents) seek work from beginning writers that is complete or near complete. Ask in your letter if the agent would be interested in seeing part or all of your novel or book.

Likely, you'll receive word back in two to three weeks. Send your work immediately to any agent who asks to see it.

So, make sure you have a completed book when you query agents. And make sure it is polished and near ready for publication.

As for choosing an agent and signing a contract, I'll not speak much to that. You want to find an agent with some sort of track record in closing deals. On the one hand, you want agents with a long list of clients, and on the other hand, you want an agent who will pay attention to you. If you are offered a contract, ask a professor about it. Or a published author whom you know personally. Again, the *Guide to Literary Agents* has information about this.

At the end of the day, you want an agent who is clearly enthusiastic about your work, and who is likely to place it with a publisher. Pay attention to any contract offer you receive, and read the fine print.

I hope this goes without saying, but perhaps it doesn't: any agent who asks for a "reading fee" or any sort of money from you is not an agent you should spend any time with. A serious agent believes in your work, and is confident in his or her success in placing it, and of course receiving his or her 15 percent of that deal. A serious agent also believes in your long-term success as a writer, not simply placing this one book, but also placing future books with publishers.

I want to reiterate: If you're just entering a program, don't worry about agents. This information is for your future use. Concentrate on your craft and your community.

Maria Hummel

Q: What about life after the graduate degree?
A: "Most people I've known have spent the two years—after their two years in an MFA program—completing their book. That's why funding is important when you choose a program. Consider an MFA as the first or second step on the ladder, not the final rung. You won't want to come out heavily in debt with student loans. You'll want to keep writing, and that's harder when you have to work full-time, or more, paying off loans. Even some of the best writers I know succeeded in publishing their first books long after their MFA program, and it took some up to a decade to do it. . . . The MFA experience is rich and rewarding, and it also shakes you up a bit, and can confuse your perspective on your own work. Sometimes workshop can be too much response. It takes a while to let those workshop voices in your head settle down. When you begin to work in isolation again, with your own voice in your head, that's when you make your true progress."

How do I go about choosing my thesis committee?

A thesis committee is normally three professors who will read your final thesis (a book-length manuscript of your creative work) and offer questions, comments, suggestions, and insights. You'll choose your committee near the beginning of your last year in the program. Your primary thesis adviser is, obviously, the most important member of your committee. Choose someone who understands your work, is both encouraging and critical, and who will make him- or herself available for a few meetings throughout your final year.

Members of your committee are likely to be the professors in your creative writing program, but in most cases you can also choose professors from the English department, an elective department, or other professors who will have insight into your work. Your main adviser will likely be one of the fiction/poetry/nonfiction professors. Department and program chairs are often very flexible about allowing you to choose who you want.

What sort of careers do postgraduates go in to?
The creative writing degree is an artistic endeavor primarily, and a professional degree second. Graduates move on to careers in a variety of fields, but they all keep (or should keep) writing a priority in their lives. Graduates teach on the university or high school level, they become editors and Web designers, they write in the business world, they become journalists, they work as administrators in education, and sometimes they go on to other degrees in law, political science, and education.

Don't expect your degree alone to open up limitless opportunities in the teaching and publishing worlds. That said, the degree *will* open up opportunities in your creative endeavors.

And by the way, I would strongly recommend that you work as an intern during one of your summers in the program. This might be at a publishing house, a newspaper, a literary journal or other magazine, or in an educational or business setting. Working as an intern can lead to later employment, either with that organization or with another. The Associated Writing Programs (AWP) has listings of positions, as does the magazine *Poets & Writers*. Searching the Web is a good way, also, as is asking your program coordinator.

Toward the end of your first year, make an appointment with the head of the program to talk about what steps you should take to plan your professional life after graduate school.

Michael Collier

Q: What advice would you offer for postgraduates?
A: "You have to protect your identity as a writer all the time, because so many things in our culture work against being a writer. This is true for all writers, including those who have full-time work in a university. If you teach English at a high school, you have to think of yourself as a writer who happens to teach English at a high school, and not as a person who was once in a graduate program as a writer and who now teaches English in high school. It's an important distinction. . . . If you write software during the day, you have to think of yourself as a writer of poetry or fiction or nonfiction, not just at night, but all the time. Keep involved in your community of writers. Keep in contact with your classmates. Keep writing. This sense you have of yourself as a writer should override everything else. If you can't convince yourself that you're a writer, then you're not going to get the work done."

Agents, long-distance relationships, thesis committees, careers . . . my head is spinning. Can you center me in some way?
Yes I can. It's called chapter summary.

But before we get to that, relax. You're about to have a great and memorable experience in your life. Over the next few years you'll concentrate on your writing, you'll grow as a person, you'll be part of a writing community, you'll have new experiences and meet a variety of people. Work hard. Push yourself. Have fun. There's a few more stops on the tour, but that's about it for the bus driver. I hope our time together was helpful to you. I enjoyed the tour, as I always do. Get out there now and explore the city. Find what you need. Check out those side streets. Happy trails, and rock on.

Chapter Summary

1. Visit your new program before the school year begins in order to take care of housing and to meet fellow students and professors. Make residency status in your new town a priority.

2. Make sure you speak with and learn from veteran students. Meet with them, buy them a cup of coffee, ask questions, listen. They have all sorts of insights that will help you avoid pitfalls and help you make the most of your graduate experience. This is the most important advice in this chapter.

3. Take three or four classes each semester of your first year. This will help you get acclimated to the program, meet new people, and get some requirements out of the way.

4. Take part in the social aspects of your program, both formal and informal. Attend readings, seminars, parties, and other get-togethers. Keep or create outlets for yourself, outside of the program, to keep things in perspective. Take a yoga, art, or dance class. Join a gym. Take a part-time job. Make friends outside of the program. Keep in touch with old friends and, of course, your family.

5. If you value your current romantic relationship, either move together to the new town, or make plans to be together in the very near future (no longer than a year). Any lack of a plan will likely result in a lack of a relationship.

6. Set aside a place and time for your writing. Make a writing schedule and stick to it. Write everyday, for as much as five hours or as little as fifteen minutes. Don't be afraid to work on a few projects at once: this will keep your mind fresh and will prevent boredom with one single project. Seek new experiences so that you have new input for your writing. Remember that the best cure for writer's block is reading. Read a lot, then write a lot. Get feedback on your writing at appropriate times from collaborators and colleagues.

7. Get to know your professors, formally or informally. Read their work and be familiar with it. Ask for advice about your creative work and about reading lists.

8. Seek a literary agent once you have built up a body of small publications *and* when you have a larger work to sell. Seek the agents of writers who you admire and who write in a similar way to you. Send query letters and use the *Guide to Literary Agents* from Writer's Digest Books.

9. For your thesis committee, choose a primary adviser who is familiar with your work, who is encouraging and also critical. Think about whom you'd like for your committee at the beginning of your final year.

10. Graduates of creative writing programs take jobs in a variety of fields. Teaching and editing, of course, but also web design, journalism, administration, business, and, of course, many graduates go on to other advanced degrees. The creative writing degree is an artistic endeavor primarily, and a professional degree second. That said, keep an eye on your postgraduate career, especially after your first year. Seek summer internships and talk with your program director about steps to take to create career options.

CHAPTER 6A

Interview with Scott McCabe

My interview with Scott McCabe, a graduate of the Lesley University MFA program, was particularly helpful in regard to understanding low-residency Programs. I've decided to include the bulk of that interview here. Thanks, Scott.

Q: Can you talk about the structure of your low-residency program?
A: "Each semester begins with a ten-day intensive residency. We meet for workshops and seminars, and for evening readings. Then at the end of the residency, we break our own ways and work one-on-one with a faculty mentor for six months or so. There aren't really classes in the traditional sense. It's hands-on, active learning; students get to help shape their syllabi and spend much of the time teaching themselves. At Lesley University there are three lines of work: creative writing, craft reflection and annotations, and inter-disciplinary work. The interdisciplinary work is an opportunity to pursue a medium that helps inform our creative writing. Some people work in graphic design or illustration, others playwriting. A friend worked as an intern for a small local publisher. I worked on the art of the author interview, learning another way to make a living as a working writer."

Q: What are the craft reflection and annotations?
A: "I'll work independently for a month, writing and reading. I'll read two to three books in that time. The annotations are focused on craft: this or that aspect of technique. We write two to three pages and, generally, the closer the focus the better. One month I read the

collection *Werewolves in Their Youth* by Michael Chabon. He has such a hyperfluent vocabulary but sometimes he would scale the language back. Some of the descriptions were, comparatively, plain, and that plainness contrasted in such a way as to focus the reader's attention, subtly, like a whispered secret. These were some of the most important moments in the story. So, I wrote about that."

Q: What about the creative writing aspect?
A: "During that same month's time we write a minimum of fifteen pages, either new work or significant revision. You have an independent schedule so you have to motivate yourself. One of the nice things about the low-residency model is that it mirrors the life of a working writer. Someone who has to work for a living but who also has a separate creative life. It is a demanding schedule of work, and there is not a regularly meeting community of people to rely upon for support or an influx of creative energy during those dark moments I suspect all writers have, where the words have jaunted off without saying goodbye and haven't bothered to call or write to say when they can be expected back. You've got to figure a way to work through it on your own."

Q: What are the residencies like?
A: "They're very fun. You don't see these people for six months, so you look forward to it. The first couple of days there is a tangible excitement. It's nice to take time off from professional work. You dive into the writing life. The days are long, though. Craft and writing seminars in the morning, workshops in the afternoon, readings in the evening. That's every day. You have to pace yourself, otherwise you can wear down pretty fast. These take place on the Lesley campus in Cambridge. It's a very vibrant and literary community. There are lots of places to go, and things to do. That's both good and bad. You have more to do, but that can also undercut the community feel of the program. Groups of people can go their separate ways at night. If instead you were sequestered in the woods or at the top of a mountain and the resident and entertainment options limited, then there might be more of a sense of being together."

Q: What about the community of a low-residency program?
A: "You make friends and colleagues during the ten days of the residency. You can call them up after the residency is over, for advice, or

just someone to talk with about your projects. I write to a handful of people on a fairly regular basis, sometimes to talk about problems with the work, sometimes just to chat. There is also a student-run online community. A message board. There's that avenue for more wide-ranging responses."

Q: What's your daily schedule like?
A: "I'm an editorial assistant at a textbook company in downtown Boston. The job is forty hours a week, not including travel time, which, depending on the trains, is about an hour each way. It can be difficult when you come home from work. You eat, do a bit of unwinding, then you get down to your creative work."

Q: What advice would you offer to new students?
A: "The most important thing is to take a real special care in choosing your faculty and keeping in touch with them. For the six months between residencies, they are your primary link to the program. It makes a big difference, how you respond to their teaching and how they respond to your work. Before you choose, go to the library and read their work. That's tremendously helpful. Seek out those people whose work you respond to. A good mentor could be someone who simply places the right texts before you. . . . Another thing is cultivating relationships with other students. It's helpful to have those relationships and to know that they are going through the same things. It's not necessary that they're in the same genre as you. Sometimes its nice to get another perspective, the same way it is to read in another genre. Those relationships can help fill gaps that the faculty can't fill or shouldn't fill. . . . In a similar way, wherever you are locally, I think it's a good idea to attend readings and literary evens as much as possible. It keeps your creative energy up. You get involved with other writers and readers."

Scott McCabe is a graduate of the MFA program at Lesley University and Bowdoin College. His work has appeared in the *Harvard Review*.

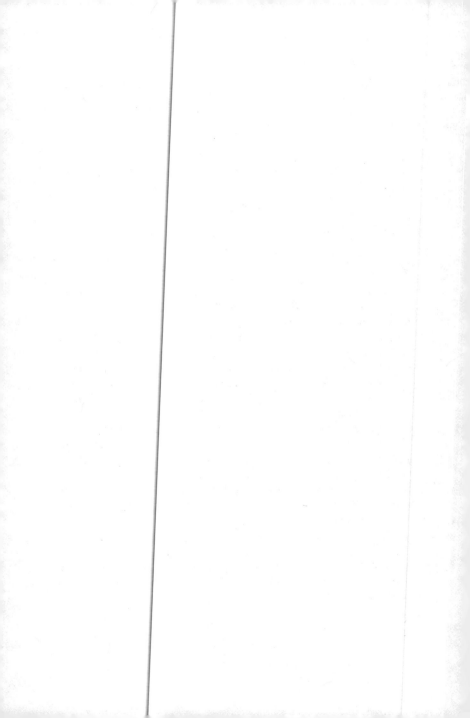

Your Teaching

THIS SHORT CHAPTER ADDRESSES QUESTIONS related to teaching composition or creative writing on the university level. It may also be helpful for graduate students who are teaching or research assistants for professors.

What can you tell me about teaching?
What I'd like to tell you about teaching would take a whole other book, so I'll try to be brief here.

There will be some sort of orientation for first-time teachers, sponsored by the program, the department, or the university. Be sure to attend this, as it will be not only smart, but required. Some orientations will last a full semester before you teach or during your first teaching semester, and others will be a few days before the first semester starts.

During the orientation you'll learn about the specific goals of your courses. You'll learn about each of the assignments you'll be teaching. (For example, at the University of Massachusetts we taught a number of papers including the personal essay, responding to text, the research paper, the persuasive essay, and others). You'll learn about which tools—group exercises, homework, conferences, peer feedback, in-class writing—you'll use to meet these goals. And, of course, you'll talk about teaching styles and methods.

We had a good orientation at the University of Massachusetts, and the most helpful aspect of the three day course was a Q&A with veteran graduate teachers. Here, we concentrated on the nuts-and-bolts of running a classroom. Questions included:

- What should I include in the syllabus?
- What kind of writing exercises should I use?
- What about my attendance policy?
- How long will it take me to grade eighteen to twenty-five papers?
- What kind of comments should I include?
- How will I encourage discussion in the class?
- Is this textbook useful, and if so, which sections are most useful?
- How many weeks should I plan ahead?
- How many weeks for each class paper?

And those are just the big-picture nuts and bolts. Some smaller, though no less important issues are: Should my students call me Mr. Kealey or Tom? What arrangement of chairs—facing the blackboard, in a circle, in small groups—is best for which days or assignments? How do I set up a library tour? What happens when I don't know the answer to a question? What happens, on a sunny day, when students ask, "Can we have class outside?"

My point? Don't count on the orientation to teach you everything, or even to teach you what you actually need to know about running a classroom.

I am *strongly* encouraging you to seek out veteran teachers and listen to what they have to say. Buy them a coffee and ask them specific questions. Good teachers are excited about teaching, and they like to talk about it. Ask a veteran teacher if you can sit in on a class. You can learn a lot by just watching. While your solutions/strategies in the classroom may be different, you can receive good insight from people who have been there and done that.

How can I balance teaching and writing?

Good question. When I was a graduate student, a professor once said to a group of us, "Do as little as you can, teaching-wise, and concentrate on your writing instead." I didn't think much of this at the time, and I still don't. However, a necessary point arises: make sure you schedule writing time, and don't allow your teaching responsibilities to infringe upon it. Remember that you'll spend a lot of time on your teaching during the weeks that papers/stories/poems are due. Schedule for that. And schedule more of your writing time for the other weeks.

I am strongly encouraging you to set up four to five blocks of time each week for your writing. Some people like to maintain a consistent schedule: Every morning for two hours. Or every evening, starting at 10 P.M., for three hours. Or all day Saturday. Try to observe your best writing times: some of us are morning people, others are night owls. I'm encouraging you to block out two to three hours, three times, during the weekdays, and a longer writing session some time over the weekends. Choose the times: say, 9 P.M. Monday nights, 8 A.M. Tuesdays and Thursdays, Saturday from noon to five. Stick to these times, and don't allow other aspects—teaching, personal, classwork—to infringe on them. You are in school to write. Make it a priority, and keep it a priority.

Can you give me some other tips about teaching?

- Try to avoid teaching Monday–Wednesday–Friday classes. Many schools have dropped this practice, and I'm not sure why all of them haven't. Try to get on a Monday–Wednesday schedule or a Tuesday–Thursday schedule. Why? Because it will allow more time for your writing and,. more important, you can do more with two hour-and-a-half classes than you can with three fifty-minute classes. Why is that? Because I said so. Learn the hard way if you like.
- The syllabus: Do ask for syllabi from veteran teachers. Try to keep your syllabus to no more than two pages. Offer a brief introduction to the class, introduce the text book, state goals, make clear the requirements, make the attendance policy clear, and offer a brief schedule.
- Why a brief schedule? You should have a rough-draft schedule of the entire semester in your own notes. Try to stick to this. In many cases, schedules will change. I used to give students the schedule for the entire semester. Then I went to half a semester. Then I went to the first six classes. Nowadays, I simply include the first three classes on the syllabus. I always tell students what the schedule will be three classes in advance, during each class, but I allow for some leeway for classes beyond that.
- I like to write the schedule for the next few classes on the board during the break in the class. This means that I've told them *and* shown them. This will save you a lot of headaches.

- Take roll at the beginning of each class. This will help you learn students' names (which you should know by the end of the second week), and it will show that you are paying attention to who is there and who is not.
- The first day of classes: I want to take attendance, pass out the syllabus, explain the syllabus, go around the room and ask them to introduce themselves in some way (be sure to ask veteran teachers about how they do this). I want to introduce the textbook, I want them to write in class in some way so that they get in to the habit of writing (ask veteran teachers about writing exercises), and I want to make the homework for the next class clear. Often, I'll let them leave early on the first day, especially since they've got a lot to do around campus. However, I make it clear that we'll stay for the full class for the remainder of the semester.
- As far as classroom discussions go, don't be afraid of the silence. By that I mean, when you ask a question of the class, wait for them to answer, even if you have to wait for a full minute. Stay quiet, and someone will eventually answer. If you get in to the habit of asking a question, pausing for a few seconds, then answering the question yourself, students will expect this pattern for the rest of the semester. In fact, they'll assume that this is the pattern you prefer. So, ask your questions, and wait for the answers. Don't be afraid of the silence.
- If you're having trouble keeping discussions going, don't be afraid to call on students directly. Often, they are simply waiting for permission to answer.
- A break: If your class will run longer than an hour and a half, allow a five-minute break. This gives you a break too, and you can reorganize for the second half of class. It allows students to go to the bathroom or simply stretch their legs. This sounds obvious to me as I write it, but a lot of teachers don't do this. You can only cram so much information in to their heads in an hour and a half. Give their brains and other body parts a break. I always start the second half exactly after five minutes. This stops five-minute breaks from stretching in to ten minutes. Students take note of your promptness.
- Try to accomplish three major things each class period. These might include a lecture about writing, a discussion about a text, an in-class writing assignment, small group work, or

introducing a new assignment. Try to keep these to no more than twenty-five minutes each. This keeps the class period rolling along, it prevents students from getting bored, and it allows you to accomplish a lot during the course of the semester. Most important, it keeps you organized. And an organized teacher is an effective teacher.

- It's your job to help students improve on their writing weaknesses and to help them correct mistakes. But it's also your job to reinforce and draw attention to the things they are doing well. Make sure you do both. The second is as important as the first.

- Always allow for in-class writing time, at least once a week. This helps them practice what you're preaching. Less important to them, but perhaps more important to you, it allows blocks of time that you don't need to intensely prepare for. Find interesting writing exercises, or give them specific assignments that are relevant to, or actually allow them to work on, their papers.

- Get to know your fellow teachers, veterans and rookies alike. You can bounce ideas off of them, trade class plans, and, perhaps most important, you will have people to decompress with after a long day or week of teaching. Just having people available who can commiserate with the same challenges and situations will help you a great deal. Try to schedule your office hours at the same time as other teachers. If no students visit, this can be prime teacher discussion time.

- Take care of yourself. Get your sleep, eat right, make time for yourself, your writing, your own classes. If you're healthy and happy, your classroom atmosphere will be the same.

Any final thoughts on teaching?

Everyone wants to take creative writing classes. They are often some of the most popular classes on campus, and there are often long waiting lists for students. Motivation in these classes is no problem.

On the other hand, no one wants to take composition classes. Some students believe they should've "placed" out of them, other students think writing is boring, and a good number of students believe that they are simply not good writers, and they dread going to these classes.

That sounds depressing, but that need not be the case. Look at it this way: if you can make your class fun, interesting, sometimes unpredictable, and, most important, relevant and useful to students, then they'll look at writing in a very different way. Their expectations are low for the class. I am *not* arguing that you should meet these low expectations. But I am saying, if you can make the class fun, challenging, and relevant to students you'll surprise them. A lot of their friends are taking boring classes. If yours rises above their expectations, they'll take note, and you'll have their efforts and interest.

If you believe, communicate, and project that writing is valuable and important to you, then you'll have a much easier time of teaching. And when you project that *their* writing is valuable and important to you, you'll have an even easier time.

You're not necessarily *friends* with students. (And you're certainly not their enemy). You're their teacher, guide, and mentor. But you're also a colleague of theirs, in the art and craft of writing. Be a friend of their writing, and of their class experience.

CHAPTER 6C

The Writing Workshop

Aimee Bender

Q: As a teacher, what do you expect out of your students in workshop?

A: "It's important that students turn in work that they've spent some time on. That they've thought about and rewritten. It's important that they spend time analyzing the work of their peers and that they write good critiques. To be honest, I want students to make the workshop the top priority of all their classes. Ideally, graduate students will be writing as regularly as possible. Learning and keeping some sort of writing routine is important."

This chapter addresses the creative writing workshop. Tips here for both writers and readers.

What can you tell me about the workshop?
A few things. First, the classes will hold anywhere from eight to sixteen students. Fiction and nonfiction students will be workshopped twice, while poetry students can have their work workshopped five or more times in a semester. There may be an introductory two or three classes where students read published work and discuss it, or complete short writing assignments. For the most part, however, you'll jump right in to the workshop discussion.

A workshop, as I've said, is a sort of editorial meeting about student work. A professor and the other students discuss a writer's work—its strengths and weaknesses—and offer suggestions for improvement. Meanwhile, the writer sits and listens and takes notes. Afterward, the writer can ask specific questions not covered during the workshop. Often, students and the professor will write letters to the student or make comments on the manuscript.

I have some random tips that may be of use to you.

When you are the writer:

- Never volunteer to go first. By that I mean, don't turn your story/poem in to be workshopped first. Why not? Because the class is just getting to know each other, and it's not a well-oiled machine yet. The first workshop is often, though not always, a dry run for the rest of the semester. So, if you can, hold your work back till the third or fourth workshop.
- Don't write something the night before and then turn it in the next day. We've all had strokes of genius at midnight or after. But by the light of day, the genius tends to leak away. The best writing is rewriting. So remember that a good workshop story/poem is one that has been written, has been set aside for a few days, and then is come back to with your editor's eye.
- You'll be making copies for the class for the class *before* your workshop. Make sure you leave enough time to factor for broken copy machines, long lines, and the like.
- Slackers. There are always slackers in the group who don't write letters or who offer little to no comments. If someone slacks off on my work, then I slack off on theirs. I pay attention to the writers in class who pay attention to me. Generally, I'll give my best effort the first time around, then I make changes accordingly. Keep in mind that shy or introverted students may not say much in class, but may offer outstanding and insightful written comments.
- Finally, and perhaps most important, be a stenographer when your own writing is being workshopped. I like to write down everything, or as close to everything, that is said in my workshop. I'll write a person's name and then their comment, and then on to the next person. Why? Two reasons: First, you'll

have a written record of what was said. This is important, as one strong comment in class may distract you from equally or more useful earlier comments. When you have the written record, you have notes from which to work. And second, when I concentrate on writing everyone's comments down, I concentrate less on how my work is looked upon critically or negatively. This is your baby on the table, and there will be all sorts of surprising and sometimes hurtful comments. Keep your emotions out of it by writing down all comments. Concentrate on content, not criticism.

- I like to read everyone's comments the evening after my workshop. Then I set them aside for a week, let them bounce around in my head, allow my subconscious to organize them (emphasizing some, rejecting others); and then I sit down to rewrite.
- At the end of the workshop, you'll likely be given a chance to ask questions or seek clarifications. Stick to these things. Don't explain your story or offer excuses on what you were trying to do. Comments like, "Well, what you guys obviously didn't see was . . ." are not helpful. Your poem or story either worked for this audience or it did not. It must stand on its own. Ask questions about areas that were not covered, or ask a specific student to expand a comment that was brushed over in the discussion.

When you are one of the readers:

- Don't be a know-it-all. You may see the goal of twenty-first-century poetry/fiction/nonfiction in a clear way. Others will likely see it differently. Don't impose your aesthetic on the rest of the class. A workshop is all about the work you have before you. Work to understand what it is, and what the author is trying to achieve. Keep your comments limited within this parameter. By all means, do suggest improvements or ways of thinking that the author may not be aware of. But don't impose your style on another writer.
- In general, workshop is not about right and wrong. It's about offering options to the writer. Suggestions, not demands. So avoid personal arguments with other workshop people. Argue ideas, not personalities.

- On that note, be prepared for others to object to or argue with your comments. Let them. While you may feel the need to clarify or reinforce, keep such to a minimum. This is not a courtroom. You've offered your options. If you've stated them clearly and effectively, then the writer will take note. The readers in a workshop may end up learning a lot, but remember that the workshop is primarily for the benefit of the writer.
- Don't talk to the writer. As a general rule, the writer of the work will remain silent during workshop. So, it does no good to say, "Gen, I wondered why you included this information about the mother so soon." Instead, aim your questions and comments to the teacher or to the class as a whole.
- Don't spend time talking about grammar. A misspelling or a misuse of a word can easily be marked on the manuscript, for the writer to read later. A workshop will be anywhere from ten to fifty minutes. Either way, time is precious. Stick to the structure, form, and content of the work. Offer options to the writer. If a grammar error is consistent throughout the work, then you might point it out in a small comment.
- Do offer strength assessment. Yes, you are pointing out shortcomings of the work, but it is equally important to reinforce the aspects that are working well in a story or poem. Be sure to comment on these. Often, and appropriately, strength assessment is offered at the beginning of a workshop. Typically, if the stronger aspects of a work are not praised early, then the workshop tends to forget about them.
- Letters. I always write letters in my fiction workshops. These can be handwritten, though typed is preferred. Generally, notes for shorter poetry works will be on the page of the work. The workshop leader will likely give instructions on his or her preference. In any case, be a good letter writer. Reinforce three aspects that are working well, and offer three recommendations for improvement. Spend some time on each of these aspects. When you write good letters, you'll likely receive good letters in return.
- Keep your verbal comments specific, and offer examples if possible. Keep your comments to around thirty seconds each, and no more than a minute. Be clear and concise. Writing your letter or your written comments should give you an idea of your best suggestions. Don't be afraid to give your overall

impression of the work—talk about what it is and what it's trying to do—but keep the majority of your comments specific, useful, and applicable.

Any final comments about workshop?

Yes. My colleague at UMass, Nick Montemarano, used to tell me this: When you're the writer in workshop, it's like driving a car with twelve people in the backseat, all of them telling you which way to go. They all may actually be giving good directions and driving instructions, but if you listen to all of them, you're likely to crash the car. Be sure to pick out a few specific voices. Who best understands what you're trying to do with a work? Who gives the best insights? Who defends the aspects that are most dear to you? This is another good reason for not going first in a workshop. You can observe how individuals treat others' work on the table. By the end of your first year, you should have a good idea about who understands and values your work and who doesn't. Pay much more attention to the former and less to the latter.

Publishing in Literary Magazines

THIS CHAPTER OFFERS INSIGHTS AND TIPS on publishing your work in literary magazines and journals.

What about publishing? Should I be submitting my work to magazines and journals?

Definitely yes. Send out work that is polished and in your view, complete. Work that has been workshopped and edited to your satisfaction. Some tips on sending work:

- There are somewhere short of three hundred national literary magazines in the United States. They each publish some combination of fiction, poetry, essays, reviews, and artwork.
- *Writer's Market, Poets Market*, and *Novel and Short Story Market* are the three guides for researching publishing in magazines. They list all magazines accepting open submissions, and they will provide submission information, advice, and addresses. Buy them and read them. They're big, so read ten pages at a time. Take some notes in the margins. Part of beginning the publication process is reading these books carefully, and taking notes as to which magazines might be a good fit for your work.
- Look for magazines that are established and are looking for work similar to yours. Go to your local bookstore and read literary magazines. Find journals that you like, and send to those.
- One tip I've often heard: look at the poetry books or story collections of your favorite authors. Often there are lists of

magazines where the work was previously published. This is often found on the copyright or acknowledgments page. Consider these magazines for your work.

- Also, consider *The Best American* series (stories, poetry, non-fiction, etc.). There are lists of magazines at the back of these books and citations for the work included.

- A very incomplete list, but a starting point nonetheless is: *Story Quarterly, Poetry, Tin House, Glimmer Train, Pleiades, American Poetry Review, Southwest Review, Zyzzyva, Virginia Quarterly Review, Missouri Review, Boulevard, Puerto del Sol, Five Points, The Sun, Georgia Review, Epoch, Field, Ploughshares, Tri Quarterly, Fiction, Prairie Schooner, Crazyhorse, Alaska Quarterly Review, Indiana Review, Witness, Grand Street, Iowa Review, Mid-American Review, Jubilat, Meridian, Black Warrior Review, Michigan Quarterly Review, Chicago Review, Southern Review, Fiction, Seattle Review, New England Review, Quarterly West, North American Review, Third Coast, and Gulf Coast.* And, some of the big ones: *Atlantic, Harper's, Paris Review, McSweeney's,* and *Zoetrope.*

- Do your research, and don't limit yourself to these. There are many fine magazines out there.

- Consult websites that list links to magazines. I've listed these in appendix B.

- Consult veteran students and professors about where to send work.

- Generally speaking, magazines are looking for stories in the 3,000- 5,000-word range. Magazines look for poetry in the one- to five-page range. Many publications actively seek new writers, so don't be intimidated if you haven't published before. Part of being a writer is sending your work out, getting rejected, revising your work, sending it out again, and getting it placed. If you can't stand rejection, look for another line of work. Sometimes your work is not ready, sometimes editors are idiots. Control what you can: revise and polish your work, study the market, then send your work out. If you receive a return letter asking for revisions, then revise and resend within a month's time.

- Send one story at a time to a magazine, or three to five poems.

- The manuscript: No crazy fonts or wacky pagination. Use the Times New Roman font (or the like). No title pages. Number your pages, especially in the case of fiction. Staple or paper clip your work. Put your name on page 1, and I like to put my name and e-mail address on the last page of my stories. Some magazines are notorious for losing your accompanying letter. If a publisher wants your poem or story, make sure they can get in contact with you.

- Of course, many magazines now accept submissions online. This is a great time- and postage-saving technological advance. Magazines will normally get back to you in less time when they accept submissions online.

- Generally speaking, magazines will reply in three months' time.

- Simultaneous submissions: Some magazines do not accept submissions that you've also sent elsewhere. I think this is stupid. You can't afford to send a poem out, wait three or more months (sometimes as long as six to eight months), get rejected, and then send it out again, only to wait for another half year. I avoid simultaneous submission magazines, and you should too. Some magazines say, "Simultaneous is okay, as long as you let us know, and as long as you contact us if a piece is accepted elsewhere." This seems fair to me, and you should honor that request.

- That said, how many magazines should you send one work to? My answer: around six at a time. Spread your net wide.

- And, that said, *make sure* you keep track of where and when you've sent your work. Write it down in your notebook or in a computer file. Update it as your are accepted and rejected. Don't make the mistake of sending a rejected work to the *same* magazine later.

- I've had stories that were rejected eight times by varying publishers, then accepted somewhere else. Keep sending out your work. If a work is rejected, say, a dozen times, then it likely needs to be set aside and edited. You can't account for editors' tastes and opinions, but you can polish or rework your poems/ stories when necessary.

- The accompanying letter: Make it formal. Include the magazine's address and your address. If at all possible, find the name of the fiction editor and address the letter to him or her. If not, "Fiction Editor" will do. Don't explain your poem or story. If you have previous publications, list them in your letter. If you are in a writing program, state that. Before I was published I simply wrote "Here's a story," and I was accepted at a number of places. Be direct and brief. Your story has to stand on its own. Before you send out your first letter, show it to those who have had success in getting published. Follow their advice.

- Other advice: When sending via post (snail mail), always, always, always include a self-addressed stamped envelope (SASE).

- Sometimes you get paid, sometimes you don't. I've been paid as much as $500 and as little as two copies of the magazine. You're trying to get your work and your name out there for people to see. Don't worry about the money.

- I'd say that I've sent about 120 copies (total) of around twenty original stories. Twelve of my stories were accepted. That means about 10% of the time I've dropped something in the mail, it's been taken. It also means that 90% of the time, the work has not been accepted. That's manageable for me, and seems—give or take a few percentage points—what my colleagues have experienced as well. My point? Expect to be rejected, and keep sending. One work placed for ten sent out is workable. Often, the majority of rejections will come as you first send your work.

- Keep sending. Persistence and patience counts for everything in the writing world.

So You've Got an MFA. Now What?

by Adam Johnson

OKAY, LET'S SAY YOU GO GET THAT MFA. You spend a couple years writing your heart out—you make leaps, discoveries, have insights, and maybe publish a piece or two. Perhaps you even find your voice. You bond with a couple writers who "get" your writing, and you know you'll share your work with them forever. You've read widely across other centuries and cultures and are a more thoughtful critic and generally better human being because of it. Along the way, there are celebrations, opportunities for growth, and more than one romance. For a couple years, you manage to meditate and work out every single day. Then you turn in your thesis (a truly glorious piece of writing, I might add) and as the English department softball season winds to a close and the whir of the margarita blender begins to fade, you are faced with this question: What the heck is next? Do you move to New York to live off your royalties or move back home with your folks? Do you return to your old waiter's job, wearing your thick new eyeglasses and your sporty carpal tunnel braces? Do you go get another MFA or, god forbid, a PhD? The answer depends on why you wanted an MFA in the first place.

Before we continue, full disclosure: I have an MA, an MFA, and a PhD.

If you decided to get an MFA because, after your bachelor's degree, you were lost, lazy, or unsure, well, you're back in the same boat. People get MFAs for other equally bad reasons: to avoid paying student loans, to continue qualifying for a trust fund or to avoid mandatory military service in the nation of your birth. Well, maybe avoiding military service in the nation of your birth isn't such a bad reason to get an MFA. I must admit that, when applying for MFA programs, I visualized myself in the air conditioning for a couple years.

The worst reason to get an MFA is to avoid real life. The whole reason to learn to write is so you'll have the skills to tell a personal story, one that was lived. Also, if you haven't lived, there's a danger that you might come to believe that an MFA program is real life. Any graduate degree involves lots of work and self-sacrifice, but in general, you'll be breathing rarified air for a couple years. Being in an MFA program is like living in a sci-fi biosphere on an alien planet, where everyone shares your obscure visionary notions—namely, that literature matters, that English professors know more than other people, that typing, alone, in your underwear, is what everyone should be doing on a Friday night. Better to tell your first post-MFA boss that you speak Klingon in your spare time. There are few great stories in the taxpayer-funded, bureaucratic realm of higher education, but even if you find a good one—do other people want to read it? Do *you* want to read a story set in an English department?

The easiest solution to this post-MFA scenario is to get out in the world and live a little. Before you head off for that master's degree, I suggest you hitch up with the Immigration Service as a border patrol agent. Sign a year contract. After twelve weeks of intensive training in Yuma, Arizona, you'll be assigned to jewel towns like Sierra Vista or Calexico. Before you know it, you'll be rolling old school in a mint-green blazer uplinked to a Blackhawk helicopter that will do your bidding. You'll have night vision goggles, infrared trackers, and before you know it, you'll be pointing your Maglite across the arroyo at another living, breathing human being. You lock eyes, and I tell you, greenhorn, there's a whole novel in that moment. Plus, you get benefits and vacation. Okay, okay, I'm from Arizona, so I'm partial to jobs that include pistols and Big Gulps. The point is that poetry and fiction are composed of images and details. Authority comes from here, and the definition of a good image or detail is that thing you couldn't make up, that observation that had to be witnessed and reported, the thing the reader believes *couldn't* be concocted. You need to train your eye to observe these before you can become proficient at concocting them.

I suppose firearms aren't necessary to get real-life details. A job as a restaurant inspector will do, even the vainglorious EMT position. Have you considered delivering oxygen tanks? The job doesn't matter as long as you come in contact with real people in situations where something's at stake.

If you're going to take a couple years off between your undergraduate and graduate degrees for the express purpose of "living life," I suggest you work rather than traveling to Prague to live on Marlboros and sangria, let alone joining the Peace Corps. If you're looking to simply take notes on your fellow humans, sit on a bench in the mall. Work is about labor and locomotion, about personal industry, about taking a position within a larger system. If you work, avoid selling things and be leery of all-consuming jobs like cruise ship work. Steer clear of taking jobs where others recreate; it's easy to come under the spell that you, too, are having fun. This rules out bars, hotels, casinos, ski slopes, and so on. Most jobs that come with a uniform are safe. Carry a clipboard. Buy a thermos. Pack your lunch.

Wait—wasn't this essay assuming you already have an MFA? Let's also assume you sought yours for noble reasons. The most noble one is the most selfish: that you adore writing, and you know that you'd never regret dedicating a couple years of your life to the thing about which you are most passionate. This conception of an MFA is based on service, that you want to live in servitude of this mysterious thing called writing that's taken hold of your heart. Basically, it's deciding to live the writer's life temporarily in the hopes that it becomes permanent. This means writing every day, devouring books, drafting, listening to the advice of others, and taking risks with your work. And, of course, there's a professional dimension. I've been emphasizing the importance of knowing the working world before you undertake an MFA because it's a tremendous amount of work. To earn your degree, you'll be asked to complete a book-length project, which will require deadlines, late nights, word counts, and timelines. And don't forget: you'll be balancing teaching, graduate courses, and your thesis. It may seem that all this work is adversarial to living the writer's life, but teaching writing and studying writing at least elucidate and inspire. And it's controlled adversity, applied with the hope that you'll thrive in its face. (As opposed to trying to live the writer's life while you frame houses during the day and bartend at night.)

The other noble reason to seek an MFA is to enlist a mentor. As an undergraduate, you get small connections with instructors, usually lasting no more than a semester or two. I advocate under-graduate writing students take as many different writing instructors as possible so they can become familiar to the range of insightful response to their work. For a graduate student, it's just the opposite. The point of seeking an MFA is to apprentice yourself to a writer you admire. By taking you on as a protégé, the writer agrees to make you a years-long personal project, reading everything that you write in the hopes of personally charting the growth of your voice. In return, you treat this mentor like a god.

This is a rare and special relationship, one that exists in precious few places outside the American university. There's simply no other socially acceptable way to establish a relationship with writers, aside from stalking their laudromats or ambushing them outside their therapists' offices. Send your favorite writer a fan letter and you'll probably get a nice, brief note in response. Send your favorite writer a six-hundred-page handwritten novel and see what happens. Forget about asking that writer to read everything you compose for a couple years. When you ask a stranger for that kind of commitment, you're asking for a relationship, and generally, asking strangers for extended relationships ends in moments of tenderness like a chemical spray or a court-ordered evaluation. So it is to the English department that you must go to commandeer the time of a writer who's actually written a body of work. The first meeting with your mentor the English department mailroom is likely to be just as awkward as on the street, but remember: here the writer (now a professor) is getting 401k benefits to talk to you. It's a perfect match, as there are few ways for writers to make a living beyond the fat of a state-run bureaucracy, and most writers I've met have amazing stories of their own mentorship by other writers, and I think most successful writers are looking for ways to give back. The MFA program allows all this to happen.

There was no book like this when I went off to pursue a writer's life. I'd been a lame student in high school, one whose motto was "C's get degrees." I soon became a shoring carpenter, and my path in the few years it took me to get to college was pocked with bridges, pump stations, and midrises. My lone literary influence during this time was a millwright who lived in his van in the parking lot of a chemical plant we were building in Chandler, Arizona. He wrote haiku all day and kept a pistol-gripped, sawed-off shotgun in his toolbox, each barrel of which was loaded with a half roll of dimes—for "crowd disbursement," he said. I only remember one of his haikus:

Oh, the cry of the
cricket, caught in the hawk's beak.
I hammer my thumb.

And a couple years later I was working on the eighth deck of the Scottsdale Hilton when I had one of my two epiphanies so far in life. Gerry, the tower crane operator, liked to eat KFC all day long at the controls. He was an expert at how wind and speed and gravity exerted themselves in the space below him, so he could toss a drumstick from the boomhouse with wicked accuracy, and, with twenty stories to freefall, incredible velocity. The decks, as we built them, were marked with large grease stains of his near misses. One day I was crossing the freshly cured concrete deck with a worm-drive Skilsaw in my hand, daydreaming about something or other. Then my knees went out from under me. It was as if a great fist had come down. The impact scored a deep red line on my forehead from the hardhat webbing, and as I dusted myself off and pieced things together, it was like I was a character in a bad novel: "Adam Johnson rose from the hardened plane, and shaking his fist at the sky, let the world know he was headed to college where he would sit in the air conditioning all day." Of course I didn't quit for a few more months—that's how epiphanies really work—time enough to see a tragic accident unfold on the job site: Gerry, instead of climbing down and up twenty flights of stairs every time he needed to use the bathroom, urinated in a gallon milk jug, which he kept on the boom of the crane—out in the Arizona sun. An emergency braking maneuver shook the jug off the crane, launching a hot urine bomb that, when it detonated hundreds of feet below, nearly killed a man. The incident ended with a pistol.

My second epiphany came when I was in a fiction writing class at Arizona State University. I'd made it to college, but was an older student, and not a very good one. I excelled at easy courses, including History of Music, Jazz Influences, and Family Studies, which you watched once a week on TV. Finally, a friend told me that creative writing was the easiest A on campus. That's how I found myself in the class of Ron Carlson, one of this generation's marquee practitioners of the short story. Suddenly, all the "flaws" I'd been told

I'd had—daydreaming, lying, rubbernecking, exaggeration—all combined to make something good: a short story, which was technically a work of art, and in my Art Appreciation class, it was made clear to us that creating art was like the highest, most lasting thing a person could do. I was hooked.

I began writing short stories at night, where I worked as a doorman at a nightclub. Summers, I kept a notepad in my toolbelt and took notes with a square carpenter's pencil. I pioneered a writing technique by which stories were composed on legal pads while driving at high speeds across the Sonoran Desert. The theory was that the conscious mind, occupied with steering and so on, would free the darkest part of my soul to emerge on the page. Yes, I'd been reading Conrad, and I never solved the serious penmanship issues that came with drive-writing. My roommates were getting worried; I'd head off to my room to write when it was obvious that a keg had just been tapped. My girlfriend didn't "get" my stories. She had to go.

For all my ambition, it was hard to produce satisfying work. My writing wasn't good—wouldn't be for a while, mind you. I just knew it could be better, but I didn't know how, and I was left unsatisfied, especially when I began working full-time. I was trying, but failing to thrive. I felt like Dante did when he strayed from the path and encountered the She-Wolf of Incontinence. What Dante needed was Virgil.

For me, wanting an MFA was a no-brainer. I didn't have fantasies of being a literary star—I just wanted to live the life, to be in the game. I wanted to commune with other writers as well. There were cool writers at ASU, but MFA students don't tend to hang out with undergrads, and my fellow undergrads looked at me with suspicion: I was older, wore workboots to class and it was obvious I'd never seen a Kurosawa movie. Okay, I also had a mullet haircut. And maybe I had some hygiene issues.

I applied to ten schools and was accepted to six, including one that was supposed to be the best. Honestly, my applications were shots in the dark. I'd never even been to some of the states where the programs were, let alone knew of the writers who taught at them. I asked people's opinions, but only became less sure of choices based on rumor and suggestion. Fretting about my decision, people consoled me with lines like, "If writing is what you love, you'll be happy anywhere you end up." But I didn't want to be happy. I wanted to be a better writer. I wanted to learn new skills, to be challenged by my peers, to have a mentor help me make "that leap" everyone was talking about.

I called one MFA program and got the name of a current student; he supposed his program was "pretty cool" but he sounded a little aloof and noncommittal. He used the word "ameliorate," which I had to look up. Wouldn't the MFA program give me the name of their most excited student? Was he a reason to rule that program out? I had no way of knowing. I found a cheap plane ticket and flew to the East Coast to meet with the director of another MFA program. I had a six-hour turnaround, so I rented a car, drove to the university, and—the director didn't show up. I sat alone in an English department hallway for two hours and then flew home. That *was* a reason to rule a program out.

Where was *this* book when I needed it?

At the time, I was reading a collection of short stories by Robert Olen Butler. It was called *A Good Scent from a Strange Mountain*, and it was to win the Pulitzer Prize later in the year. I was in love with the stories, all written in the first person with the kind of heart and voice that I was striving for. Butler's bio said he taught at a small MFA program in Louisiana at McNeese State University, and I noticed the book's dedication was to another teacher in the MFA program—a good sign, I thought. I called the program, and they gave me Butler's home phone number. Butler said to send him a story, and the next week he called me back with a response to my work that blew me away. This brings me to my main piece of advice for all prospectors of graduate programs, be they MA, MFA, or PhD: seek the mentor first and above all. Is Tim O'Brien your biggest influence? Do you love George Saunders? Do you want to be Lorrie Moore? These writers are all currently teaching at MFA programs. Forget about a program's reputation, geography, and entrance requirements. Make a list of the writers you admire and discover where they teach. Make contact, if possible. Then, grail-like, seek your mentor.

I went to McNeese State, a three-year program that conferred both an MA and an MFA. It was the right decision. Butler was a visionary teacher with a unified field theory of how literary fiction worked, and honestly, I don't know how a person could settle into the writer's life and begin to form a relationship with his or her work in less than three years. It took me a year to truly absorb the ideas I was exposed to, and other year to put them into practice. By the end of my second year, I was writing competent stories, a couple of which were published, that had little to do with me. It was in my last year that I made the leap I'd been hoping for: I began writing a different kind of story, one in which I felt spookily exposed on the page. I'd finally managed to merge what *I* cared about with what a narrator cared about, creating a character that was of me and apart from me, that allowed me to recognize myself and still make discoveries.

Then disaster struck. I graduated. I actually earned my MFA and was out on my ass just when I wanted nothing more than to redouble my writing efforts. My dream of being a daily, working writer was slipping away. Sure, I could go back to the kinds of jobs I had before, but my productivity was going to plummet. I found myself fantasizing about situations that would give me unlimited time to write. Perhaps I could read instruments at an Antarctic research facility. Wasn't there some brainwave experiment that needed a volunteer to live in a cave for a year? I literally had a dream in which I was on the space station *Mir*. I had a frustrating time eating the powdered food and urinating into the plastic tube, but floating through the capsule were all these beautiful space-age pens, more than I could ever use. Yes, I was cracking up; quickly, I began applying for PhD programs.

This post-MFA option has become increasingly popular in the past decade for just these reasons. Namely, that a writer with some ability and some promise has little recourse in the world. If you work full-time, your art is in constant danger of becoming a hobby, or worse, a diverting escape. Writers, unfortunately, are valued about as much as harpsichordists today, and like harpsichordists, they find support under the conservatory auspices of the university. That said, in your transition to life as working writer, the PhD is a nice middle step: still structured and supportive, but much more independent.

Completing the MFA, you've hopefully had a mentor and an environment where you take risks with form and subject matter. You've had a community that helped you figure things out and let you know when you hit the mark (and when you didn't). After the MFA, you need support more than mentorship, time more than feedback and independence more than supervision, so you'll have the freedom to undertake bigger projects.

I applied to six PhD programs and was accepted to four. But, as with my MFA, I found my way more through a person than an application. I'd been a big fan of *Writing Fiction*, probably the smartest book out there on narrative technique. It was written by Janet Burroway, who taught at Florida State University in Tallahassee. That's where I went, and Burroway became my major professor, directing a dissertation that I eventually published under the title *Emporium*. While an MFA mentor is often like a seasoned platoon commander who keeps you on mission, a PhD mentor is someone you seek out when you need advice, like an oracle who watches over you and dispenses wisdom just when you need it.

As a PhD student, you're on your way, rather than finding it, yet you haven't arrived, as your professors have. It can be a strange middle ground. Your writing gets workshopped harder than Master's students' work, and because you've been at this longer, you're expected to publish and succeed. On the other hand, it seemed to me that the PhD students got the lion's share of recognition, financial support, and good classes to teach. That's something to think about if you're heading off to a program that hosts masters and doctoral students side by side.

Finally, while it's possible to see an MFA as a couple-year vacation to the beloved isles of writing, the PhD will take you at least four years to complete, and it's hard not to see parallels with the monastery. First, there's the vow of poverty that you're basically taking. And don't forget the purgatorial architecture of your typical English building. You've got to read a lot of obscure texts and fulfill a translation requirement. And of course, there's blind devotion, angry questioning, and, hopefully, a vision or two.

While there's an element of play theory to the MFA, the PhD requires more serious survival skills. Here are some that I recommend: Attend all reading receptions with baggies in your pockets so you can load up on cheese cubes and boiled shrimp. Feel no shame about stealing toilet paper from the faculty bathroom. In times of crisis, avail yourself of the six free psychotherapy sessions most universities provide. Steal the copy machine codes from all of your peers and slip all your fiction submissions into the English department mail cart. Keep at least two stories in the mail to six different publications at all time. Go to half the parties, attend all the readings, and write twice as much as everyone else. Never forget that you're living your dream, something most people would kill for.

And what did I do when I finished my PhD? I began applying for fellowships.

Adam Johnson holds an MFA from McNeese State University and a PhD from Florida State University. He currently teaches at Stanford University, where he was a Wallace Stegner Fellow and Jones Lecturer. He is the author of the novel *Parasites Like Us* and the story collection *Emporium*.

APPENDIX A

Interviews

Of course, you've seen short quotes from these program directors, professors, and students throughout the book. It would be a huge mistake to not include the rest of their responses from the interviews. Much to learn here, for prospective students and others.

༄

Aimee Bender is a professor of English at the University of Southern California. She received an MFA in fiction from the University of California–Irvine. Her works include *The Girl in the Flammable Skirt* and *An Invisible Sign of My Own*. Her fiction has also appeared in the *Pushcart Prize*, *McSweeney's*, *Harpers*, and the *Paris Review*.

Q: How do you weigh the different aspects of the PhD application?
A: "I read the creative sample first. Then the critical sample and the personal statement. The creative sample is the major factor, but we'll talk about the whole package. The GRE scores round out the picture. If we're looking for amazing in one area, it's the creative work."

Q: How important is teaching experience to a writer's experience?
A: "They are definitely separate from each other. I don't think the teaching is necessarily helpful to the work of writer. Teaching is helpful for teaching experience. Some people I've known are overwhelmed by the time commitment. To me, it's a parallel interest. I like teaching and I like writing, but they're separate. Teaching helps remind me what's important in writing, so in that way it's useful, but it's not the

only way to be reminded of that. . . . Of course, an important aspect of teaching is that you get money for it. That's important to anyone."

Q: What do teachers want for and from their students?
A: "That's a good question. I want them to become more particular, more distinct in their work. I want them to go deep and to take risks. I want to give them a protected space so they can do these things. I want to encourage those risks. I want them to have funding. I want them to have as much time as they can. From them, I want motivation and a commitment to the workshop. I want them to have some sense of what they're doing, but I want an open mind, too. Sometimes graduate students come in thinking they already know what they want to do. It's a tricky balance, to be open to learning. You have to be both open-minded and stubborn. You want your writing to change. Change is exciting. You have to be open to breaking your writing apart, and then stubborn about putting it back together the way you want."

Q: Did your writing change during your graduate years, and if so, in what way?
A: "Yes, it's true that my writing changed. I was encouraged to write more fairy tale–like things, and that was incredibly liberating for me. That encouragement came from both the professors and the other writers in the workshop. I remember watching everyone else's work change. We talked a lot in workshop about the fallback position, a writing place that is too safe. Writing what is reliable. But if you feel supported, you can push past that fallback position and do something different. I remember one colleague whose novel was so different from his short stories. It was a radical and beautiful thing. . . . We were given the expectation that each of us could write even better than we already were. There was a sense that there was a higher standard. As a teacher I aspire to that now. The bar that I hold up for my students comes from a desire to help them make their writing more than it is, and more than they think it could be."

❧

Tracy K. Smith is a professor of English at the University of Pittsburgh. She received her MFA from Columbia University and was a Wallace Stegner Fellow at Stanford University. *The Body's*

Question **is her first book of poetry, and her work has appeared in**
Poetry 30, Poetry Daily, Callaloo, the Nebraska Review, Gulf Coast,
and elsewhere.

Q: How important was "place" in your selection of a graduate
program?
A: "One of the big benefits for me, in New York City, was the
vital literary scene. On any given night you could choose from a
variety of readings and even participate in some of them. I met
people inside the program, I met people outside of the program. I'd
encourage students to consider whether there will be a community
outside of their program. When you're a student, so much hinges
on the courses you take in your particular field, but your work ought
also to be based on everything that happens to and interests you as
a person. Everything impacts you in some way. New York reminded
me of that, and gave me more material to grapple with."

Q: Where should a student "be" in his or her writing career when
applying to graduate programs?
A: "It varies. You can learn something valuable at different stages
of your life. My one year off from college gave me renewed vigor
toward learning. I'd dive into my assignments. People who come
straight out of college can arrive at grad school with a sense of con-
tinuity. And people with years off from school have new material
to grapple with. It depends most on the desire you have for writing.
It's more of a question of what's going on for you and the necessity
that your work is based on. It depends more on your inner world
than the outside world."

Q: Can you talk about what students should and should not expect
from a graduate program?
A: "I think that the big thing students shouldn't necessarily expect is
a career. You go in thinking that you're automatically going to get a
teaching position and a book when you graduate with an MFA. But
in reality, it's a much longer road than that. What's more important
is the idea of community and friendship with people who are interested in the same things. You're seeking a set of readers whom you
trust with your work. You're looking for new directions in which to
read. You want mentors and faculty who can see what you're striving toward. I thought I'd be the kid at twenty-five who comes out of

grad school with a book. Instead, I had to develop more devotion to writing, more commitment. The MFA environment and the time afterward created a sense of necessity for me as a poet."

Q: Where does funding fit in to criteria?
A: "Ideally I would make my list of schools based on place and the people teaching there. Then I would make a realistic choice based on what I could afford. I went into a lot of debt, and that might be a little crazy. But I got so much out of my experience in an MFA program that I don't regret it. There are other ways to approach funding. One person I went to school with had a Jacob Javits Fellowship, so he was funded from outside the university. Exploring all of those options is a wise idea. My advice? Make funding as much of a factor as it needs to be."

Q: Any advice on the workshop experience?
A: "I have an extreme regret for workshops where people feel the need to display the knowledge they have under their belt by breaking down other writers. It happens, I think, because of their own insecurity, their own need for status. It's hard on the person being ripped to shreds, but it's also hard on the person who is aggressive in that way. We had a person like that in my incoming class at Columbia, and all he did was create a quick exit for himself from our community. He missed out on the support we gave one another. He was not part of what the rest of us were. It's important to listen to what each poet's work seems to be striving toward. Listen to what the voice is based on and what the poet is interested in. Guide your comments in that direction. If you can find a way of empathizing with that, of stepping inside it, even if it's detached from what you're used to, it broadens your own sense of possibilities. I think a workshop is most helpful when that generosity is available."

Q: How does teaching experience fit with the graduate experience?
A: "There's always something good about it. When you teach while you're young, you get a sense of whether or not teaching is ultimately what you want to do. I don't think it's absolutely imperative, though. If you want to teach, the MFA, even without teaching experience, makes you a good candidate for teaching creative writing or even composition. Sometimes waiting a little longer to teach

can be helpful. Waiting a little while before becoming a teacher gave me time to clarify and develop the ideas that were important to me as a student, and test them, try them on, before I had to formulate me into a specific set of teaching tools. I could explore more. Another thing to remember is: teaching is not restricted to the college level. You can get valuable experience out in the community working with younger or older populations."

ॐ

Rachel Kadish teaches in the MFA program at Lesley University and is a graduate of the MA program in creative writing at New York University. Her novels include *From a Sealed Room* and *Soon Also for You*. She is recipient of a National Endowment for the Arts Fellowship and the Koret Award for a Young Writer on Jewish Themes. Her work has also appeared in *Best American Short Stories* and *The Pushcart Prize*.

Q: Can you explain the teacher/student interaction in your low-residency experience?

A: "I write very detailed comments on their stories and responses. The student writes responses to what he or she has read. We stick to the plan. Or, we change it, but we both agree on this. I might say, 'I see you've taken a different turn in your writing, so let's start something new now, or revise, or try these readings.' It's a very flexible form of teaching. You can tailor the assignments for each student. I work with four students each semester. On of the things I like is that we can pivot on a dime if we choose. That's hard to do in a class of twelve or twenty."

Q: What criteria should students use in selecting an MFA program?

A: "There are two that are important to me personally. The funding issue is, I think, a prerequisite. I personally don't believe in going into debt to go to a creative writing graduate school. It's not like an MBA. You won't necessarily earn the money back in the two years after school, and you don't want to obligate yourself to taking a post-MFA job that won't allow you to write. So I tend to counsel people to not go into debt. Having said that, the most important thing for me is faculty. Don't just look at the list of faculty, but call up the program and find out who will actually *be there* during those years. They might list your favorite writer, but he or she may have only taught there for one year. Find out about the faculty you'll get to work with. Some of the best teachers I've had were not such big names at the time. You go to the library and scan their novels and see if you want to learn from this person."

Q: What about your experience in choosing a program?
A: "I guess my experience was not normal. I was living overseas at the time, not sure what I was going to do. I was dating someone who could only live in three cities: New York, Los Angeles, and Cincinnati. I only applied to two graduate programs and two PhD programs. I chose NYU because location-wise it worked, and because I'd always wanted to be a graduate student in New York City. Of course, I broke up with the guy before the summer was over. But New York University worked well for me."

Q: What advice would you offer for "getting the writing done"?
A: "You definitely have to power through it. You need to know what works for you. I need structure, and deadlines. I create deadlines, even artificial ones. I promise something to someone for a certain date. It's important to me to promise it to someone I'm a little intimidated by, or who I don't want to let down. My friend who will say, "Oh, take all the time you need" is a good friend, but he or she is not the ideal deadline person. It's helpful to me to be a little intimidated. That's just how I work. . . . Part of me appreciates the hard-ass response on that. You either get it done or you do not. I see my time differently now that I have kids. I don't answer the phone when I'm working. I don't take breaks. I don't meet another writer for coffee. You write because it makes you tick, and you write in whatever way is most effective for you. But at the end of the day I'm left with the hard-ass response: No one is going to do it for you."

Q: What overall advice would you offer to graduate students in creative writing?
A: "I feel the need to remind people that it's not an MBA or a law degree. You're growing as a writer. You're taking the degree to work on your art. You're writing within an incubator for a few years. Learn as much as you possibly can, and pick up some skills in writing, editing, and teaching. But don't put that financial

pressure on yourself that you have to have the academic job or book contract in hand. Try not to set yourself up in a financial situation so that you have to have a concrete result on the other side. Keep your debts low so that you have freedom to continue your writing."

Q: Your observations on the workshop experience?

A: "There can be some ego bruising in workshop. That's unfortunately part of the experience. No one comes out completely unscathed. Just remember, you're learning to write for the rest of your life, so look at workshop as an important part, but just a small part, of that life. Feedback is important, but not all of it is always in the best interest of the writer. You want to find one or two sympatico readers and one or two sympatico faculty. That alone is a triumph and can make a program a wonderful experience. Everything else, you get through and observe. Don't get thrown if your first workshop is not geared to the writing you like. There's the baseball analogy: getting a hit one in three times is a very good percentage."

∽

Victoria Chang holds an MFA from Warren Wilson College, and she is currently a PhD candidate at the University of Southern California. She also holds degrees from Stanford University and the University of Michigan, and works for Stanford as a business researcher and writer. Her first book of poetry is *Circle*, and she is editor of the anthology *Asian American Poetry: The Next Generation*.

Q: Like a lot of writers, you work in the business world by day, and you write creatively by night. What advice can you offer postgraduates about making a living as a writer?

A: "Yes, I am straddling two worlds. I write for a living, but it's a different kind of writing than poetry. I might eventually like to teach, though. As a writer you need to know your tolerance for living close to the poverty level. I'm probably less comfortable with it than most writers for a variety of reasons, familial and cultural pressures included. It's important to me to have a consistent income. But other people can find their own balance—it's up to the individual. For me, poetry/writing and other fields are not mutually exclusive. I think sometimes people assume that if you're not teaching writing, then you're not a writer. That's ridiculous. I have a pen, just like the next person. Society looks at you strangely when you say you're poet. That's part of the deal, but you'd be surprised at how many of my nonpoet friends are interested in reading my poetry. They're just not familiar with contemporary poetry."

Q: What are the advantages and disadvantages of a low-residency program?
A: "On the downside, it's a tough experience. You don't always get teaching training, depending on what program you're in. You're not physically near people. You lose out on a lot of interactions that residency students do receive. And the ten to twelve days you spend there twice a year are really intense. On the other hand, you get a great amount of attention from a mentor. It would be difficult for me to completely articulate how well I know my professors. You learn to write letters, which is a lost art, and you develop a deep relationship with your teacher. They were focused on me, and maybe two other students each semester. That's a lot of attention. In some ways, you find a life mentor, in addition to a writing mentor. I learned about craft for certain. But I also learned a lot about myself because of the close observations and feedback of my teachers. In addition, at low-residency programs, you have a guaranteed new teacher every semester, so if things don't work out too well, you can always count on a new teacher. This isn't always the case at residency programs."

Q: Differences between low-residency and residency programs?
A: "One thing to remember is that in a residency workshop, you spend the majority of class time working on other people's poems. In a low-residency program you concentrate on your own work. And, in many ways, you have more say over what you'll study. At many low-residency programs, you design your own curriculum."

Q: Advice on negotiating with programs about funding?
A: "State your needs and concerns. Be clear. Don't offer ultimatums, but state your individual situation. Be communicative and be open, especially once you get in. Don't assume that people know your needs. Not many people are mind readers."

Q: Thoughts on the MFA and PhD degrees?
A: "I view the MFA as an artistic degree where you learn craft.

Same thing with the PhD in creative writing. The PhD is more about learning how to be a scholar, though. I love learning. The fact of the matter is, there are things I don't know, and even more importantly, there are things I don't know that I don't know. I want to find out what those are. Curiosity is a big aspect of being a writer. My degrees in writing are furthering my own art. I'm a firm believer that critical work is deeply embedded in the creative."

Q: Advice about workshop?
A: "It's important to work within the contract of the writer within a workshop, to critique within the writer's intentions and vision. You're not trying to make their work like your work. It's key to understand what the poem is doing, or trying to do, and then you can help within that framework. Our society can be so polarized, and we see things in terms of black and white, or red and blue. We give the thumbs up or thumbs down. Literature is more complex than that, and workshop should be, too. Sometimes the most helpful feedback is to simply point out a writer's tendencies and proclivities. Helping a writer identify what it is he or she does, that's very important."

ॐ

Heather McHugh is a teacher and writer-in-residence at the University of Washington. She is also a regular summer faculty member at the Warren Wilson College for Writers. Her many works include *Hinge & Sign, The Father of the Predicaments*, and translations of *101 Poems* by Paul Celan and Euripides' *Cyclops*. She is the recipient of fellowships from the National Endowment for the Arts, the Guggenheim Foundation, and the American Academy of Arts and Sciences.

Q: Why should a student be interested in a creative writing graduate degree?
A: "In my humble opinion, one of the chief virtues of a writing program is that it buys you time to focus exclusively on your reading and writing. It is time which is formally acknowledged by the rest of the world, and that includes parents, spouses, and friends. It is time bought, not stolen."

Q: What criteria should students use in selecting programs?
A: "Two criteria would matter most to me, were I a student applying now for a residential MFA program. First, my respect for the writing of the faculty in residence. And second, my wish to reside at least for a few years in the geographical setting. This second element may matter more to me than to other people. I have to love the place where I live. It is a crucial factor in my daily equanimity."

Q: What about researching low-residency programs?
A: "I'd look at the age and venerability of the program and its academic seriousness. Does it rubber-stamp its students? Does it accept too high a proportion of its applicants? Get the scuttlebutt. One would want the most selective and most academically serious program that one could get into. [The danger is] the low-residency mode is easy to turn into a yearlong replica of the lesser writers' conferences: those that mean escape from, rather than application of, high standards. I'd contact the alumni or reunion association, former students, and ask questions about these particular issues. See how enthusiastic its alumni seem about their time in the program and their continuing contacts with it."

Q: Advice on the writing sample?
A: "Don't add drawings of flowers or unicorns. Don't indulge in a lot of fancy fonts. Don't think that imitating the work of the admitting faculty will greaten your chances. Featuring your own writing's characteristic strengths is the only way to greaten your chances. But of course, if you already know what those are, and how to feature them, you may not need an MFA program."

Q: Any advice for "getting the writing done"?
A: "If you have to ask yourself how to get writing done, you probably aren't destined to be a writer. Make yourself a good reader and count your blessings."

Q: What do students do, postgraduate? What variety of choices do students make in their postgraduate careers?
A: "I don't think postgraduate careers are usually matters of choice. Fate is the greater determiner. Most MFA graduates will not go on to teach in MFA programs. Some will, but not most. Publication will be more likely to avail in that regard. If your only ambition is to

get a job teaching in an MFA program, I'd say save your money and get yourself some prestigious publications and pray."

❧

Michael Collier is professor and codirector of the creative writing program at the University of Maryland. He is a graduate of the MFA program at the University of Arizona. His works include *The Ledge, The Neighbor, The Folded Heart, The Clasp*, and, as coeditor, *The New Bread Loaf Anthology of Contemporary American Poetry*.

Q: Can you comment on the artistic versus professional degree?
A: "An MFA is not meant to professionalize you as a writer. Rather, it is an opportunity to live as fully as possible in a community of writers for two to three years. The problem with looking at an MFA program as a professional degree is that it creates enormous distractions from concentrating on creating and establishing a discipline and identity as a writer."

Q: What questions should prospective students ask of current students?
A: "It's very important to figure out what the teaching atmosphere is like. Do students see teachers on a regular basis? Do teachers have an open door? How are students and student work handled? If you want good access to faculty, as mentors and fellow writers, then you need to know if access is available."

❧

George Saunders is a professor of creative writing at Syracuse University, where he was also an MFA student in fiction. His works include *Pastoralia, CivilWarLand in Bad Decline*, and *The Very Persistent Gappers of Frip*. His fiction has appeared in the *New Yorker, Harper's, Story*, and many other publications. He has twice won the National Magazine Award for fiction.

Q: How important is a third year of an MFA program?
A: "I think it's really important. There seems to be a cycle I've noticed. In the first year students are sizing things up. Some of

them wonder if they're good enough to belong in a program. In the second year there's usually some drama. It may be anything from workshop hostility to simply being overloaded with graduate work. But in the third year, the writing gets done. It's almost as if the first two years, you spend figuring out how to be a writer. Then in the third year you actually do it. . . . I'm definitely a big advocate of the third year. You don't want to be pushed out the door just as you're getting comfortable."

Q: Advice on choosing work for the writing sample?
A: "The holy roller answer is, 'Send your best work.' And though that is the answer, I know it's not very helpful. If it was my kid, I'd remind him that the reading period is a compressed time for faculty. We've got two weeks to read these manuscripts, six hours a day. Sorry, I don't normally read six hours a day, so it's a tough two weeks. So put your best work first. If you've got four great pages of poetry or four great pages of fiction, put those first. It's like a reality show, pitching yourself to the audience, or the girl, or the panel, or the guy in the suit. You don't have an hour. I would put the best four pages first."

Q: How much do letters of recommendation influence the committee?
A: "For the first couple of picks, we don't really worry about the letters. We feel that, if we really like the writing, the rest will take care of itself. So, you find out your number one choice is, per a letter of rec, a homicidal murderer. Well, our feeling might be, Maybe that's okay, maybe we can work with that, we can get him a little portable jail cell, whatever. For the rest, we really only look at them if it's a close call— two equally matched writers, and we can't decide. Then we try to see who might be, say, more adaptable, or who might be the harder worker. My advice is to choose three people who are going to say nice things about you, and don't worry too much about finding big names. Mostly, these letters are a way for our committee to enjoy ourselves once we make the picks. We say, 'Look, we did the right thing! Look at this letter!'"

Q: What if a student is not accepted anywhere? What advice would you offer?
A: "Yes, I'd say you definitely apply again. Not necessarily to the same programs. To some different ones, and maybe the two or three

that you really wanted to go to. I look at my own writing in my twenties, when one year I was writing very poorly and the next year I got suddenly, mysteriously better. Progress seems to happen in surges. You have to shake things up. You should get feedback on your writing, maybe take a class, definitely work on new samples for the next round. My feeling is, acceptance to an MFA program is not diagnostic in either direction. People who turn out to be great writers could be rejected, and people who turn out to be poor writers could be accepted. There are so many unknowns: How long has a writer been working on their portfolio? How old are they? Where are they in their developmental arc? I think a good deal of humility is in order in every direction. Teachers should be unsure of their own powers of selection, and writers should be humble, and hopeful, about their ability to transform their own work, suddenly, unexpectedly.... I sense that some applicants don't read much. We get a lot of TV stories. If you've been rejected, one way to shake things up is to question your reading list. Find writing that is new to you. Two or three writers that you're really excited about. Follow their lineage back. Know everything about them. Immerse yourself in those writers. For me, it was Stuart Dybek. He was from Chicago, like me. Reading him, I suddenly understood the unique power of truly contemporary literature. I felt things I hadn't ever felt before while reading. That was empowering and exciting. The thing is, if this is going to be your life, you have to go at it with everything you've got. This may be the great hidden blessing of being in an MFA program: You see that being a writer is not so rare. The deeply personal question becomes, Which writer are you going to be?"

Q: Advice on making the most of a program?
A: "Two things. First, it's not high school. It's not about the social thing, or about getting your due from the higher ups. It's not about pleasing your teacher or competing with your classmates. It's about finding your voice and getting your writing done. Second, be assertive about getting what you need from professors. We lay a lot of resources at students' feet, but we don't place those resources on their feet. It's not like they're in Paris in the 1920s, and Gertrude Stein is going to take them to lunch and make their careers. What I mean is, the writer has to be creative and assertive about making sure that whatever they need, they get. Everyone keeps office hours. The more serious students use them. They come in and ask

questions about craft or whatever's bothering them or that they're excited about. Seek mentoring. You're in charge of your resources. Think of a creative writing program as a kind of artistic Petri dish. Your job is to open your mind up and let everything in, trying not to be too judgmental. If great advice comes from a bogus, or drunken, or self-righteous, or little-published source, take it anyway."

∽✕∾

Johanna Foster is a graduate student in the creative writing program at Trinity College in Dublin, Ireland.

Q: You looked at programs both in and outside the U.S. Why?
A: "I've found that being abroad has always been powerful for me. You see life differently when you're abroad. You're more observant about people. You can't take things for granted. You get to look at language in a completely different way. You notice the language and all its quirks in greater detail. All the things that are new: these things stimulate my writing."

Q: During your research, what were some turnoffs from programs?
A: "Arrogance. I liked it when programs seemed confident about themselves. But there was often this sense—on the website, from information sessions, from administrative people and students—that their program was not only one of the best, it was better than all the rest. Some students would talk bad about other programs. 'Where else are you applying? Really? Well, they're not very good.' I would think, 'Thanks for insulting my decision-making process.' . . . In the information sessions, sometimes there was this sense, not that, 'We're a better program, and we'd like to have you,' but instead, 'We're a better program, and we thought you should know that.' That was a real turnoff. If it was meant to be a deterrent, it definitely worked."

Q: Anything else?
A: "Yes, programs who were not realistic about funding. They'd say 'You shouldn't let finances prevent you from participating in this program.' To be honest, I'd think, 'You shouldn't let this tuition prevent me from participating in this program.' Or, sometimes they were simply not forthcoming with information. Be upfront about how much it costs, and what our chances are for funding."

Q: Turn-ons?

A: "Student enthusiasm. Students who were really excited about their programs. They'd light up, talking about it. Students at Brown went out of their way. I met them through unofficial channels, through a friend, so maybe that changed things. Still, they would answer my e-mails, they'd send me invitations to readings. And it's not like Brown doesn't get enough applications. But their students seemed very dedicated to the program, and very dedicated to making it approachable."

Q: Why do you think this is the right time for a creative writing degree?

A: "To be totally honest, I wonder if it is. I thought it was. I still think it is, but I wonder. I want feedback, I want the company of other writers. I want people to read my work without me having to bake them a cake. I'm worried about when I shift my whole attention to writing. Before, it was an escape and was wonderful, now, it will be the main thing. I have a lot of self-doubt now. Is this so great because before I was doing accounting? What will I have learned when I go back to the workplace? It's tough, but at this point I'm excited about Dublin, and I'm excited about the program. People talked with a glow when they spoke about their time in the program. They said, 'That was the best year ever.' I guess I hope that is the case for me."

∽✕✑

Bruce Snider is a Jones Lecturer in Poetry at Stanford University, where he was also a Wallace Stegner Fellow. He holds an MFA in poetry and playwriting from the University of Texas Michener Center, where he later served as graduate coordinator for admissions and advising. His first book of poetry is *The Year We Studied Women*.

Q: How important is location when choosing programs?

A: "Where you're going to live is important. There are enough stresses for a writer without being miserable about your living situation. It comes down to personal preference and temperament. For me, being gay, I wanted to know if there was any kind of gay community near or at the schools. Any kind of minority community.

I didn't want to live in a conservative think tank somewhere. That mattered to me."

Q: How should students choose classes?
A: "Always talk with other students. Some programs have more flexibility in their degree plans than others. If you can take classes outside the department, take something that feeds into your work in some way. Maybe history or political science. I took a lot of film classes. Italian film, Eastern European film. I learned about how narratives are constructed visually. Also, take writing classes outside your genre. That's important. I was a poet but took fiction classes, which was very helpful. It gives you a better sense of the tools you have to work with in your particular genre, as well as the ones you don't. . . . If you have a third year and the degree plan's flexible enough, take something that'll give you another outlet. Piano, drawing, something social. One student I know took a furniture making class. He loved it. When he was struggling with his novel, he'd go to the shop and work with his hands. He solved a lot of his writing problems while building his mother a dresser."

Q: Any advice on bargaining or negotiating with programs about funding?
A: "One thing to keep in mind is that for the programs who fund all their students equally, there is nothing to bargain. Everyone gets the same thing. Otherwise, you can talk about the cost of living in that particular area. People do sometimes improve their offers by asking, but you need to be diplomatic in your approach. It's not a job offer. You should have a certain degree of modesty. Don't assume you're in some power position. No matter how good you are, you're just one person being admitted in one particular year. If you're reasonable and explain your needs, though, most programs will do what they can for you, within the bounds of their own resources."

Q: Is a third year important?
A: "Yes, I think slightly longer programs work to the student's advantage. If you're working up a manuscript, that third year makes a big difference. In some two-year programs, students sometimes feel they've spent much of that time just getting settled. In a three-year program you get two years of study and workshop, then a final

year to really work on the book. That extra year gives you a chance to put together what you've learned during the previous two."

Q: Anything to avoid with the writing sample?
A: "Basic, silly things. Don't bind your sample, don't in any way try to make it attractive with pictures, photos, drawings. Don't play with the fonts. If we received something in a binder, we threw the binder away, because we put the manuscripts into a file. You'd be surprised at how many strange things we'd get. People would bind their work into a book to make it look more 'professional.' That has the opposite effect."

Q: How important is the personal statement to the committee?
A: "The truth is the bulk of the decision is based on your writing sample, but sometimes the statement makes a difference, especially in competitive programs where the committee has to make some fine distinctions between applicants. Occasionally it helps you, but more often it hurts. Don't try to be too clever, and don't try to suck up to the faculty, and whatever you do, don't come across as arrogant. The committee can be very sensitive to these things. They'll have to work for two or three years with whomever they admit, so attitude factors in, particularly in smaller programs where's there's often less buffer between students and faculty. Be fairly direct. The committee wants to know if you're going to add something to the community, and if that something will be positive. On a very basic level, they'll want to know if you play well with others."

Q: Any overall advice on making the most of the graduate experience?
A: "No matter where you go, you can make something of it. As with most things, you can make a decision that you'll have a miserable time or an enjoyable time. You've got these two or three years to really make the most of your writing. Attend every event you can. Read everything you can. Get to know your fellow classmates. Some of these people will go on to become important readers for you even after you leave. I always found that students who took time off before they went to graduate school really appreciated it more. You know you don't always have that kind of time. . . . Also, use it as a time to take risks with your work. Often students are too

product oriented. It's okay to turn something into workshop that's an experiment, as long as you've really worked on it. The point is to become a better writer. Don't shy away from criticism. A graduate program is the place to really challenge yourself, while you have all these readers willing to tell you what they think. When you get out in the real world, editors and reviewers are not necessarily constructive. If run properly, a writing program should be."

❧

Peter Turchi directs the MFA program for writers at Warren Wilson College. He is the author of four books including *Maps of the Imagination: The Writer as Cartographer, The Girls Next Door*, and *Magician*. He is coeditor of *The Story Behind the Story: 26 Stories by Contemporary Writers and How They Work* and *Bringing the Devil to His Knees: The Craft of Fiction and the Writing Life*.

Q: What considerations should students have when researching a low-residency program?
A: "Low-residency programs typically offer a low student-to-faculty ratio, but the prospective student should learn not just how many students each faculty member will be working with but exactly what sort of relationship students have with their supervisors: how much work the supervisors read, how they respond to it, what sort of guidance is provided for the student's reading, etcetera. Do the supervisors also teach at the residency? Do students have access to other faculty at the residency? What are the opportunities for individual conferences? What sort of counseling or guidance is offered by an adviser or administrator? How is the student's work toward the degree evaluated, and how often? What are the degree requirements? Many low-residency programs look similar on the surface, just as the description of most workshops look similar; they are distinguished by how they are executed. With that in mind, prospective students should talk to current students and alumni and even, if possible, visit a residency. They might also ask how the program maintains contact with its alumni, and what alumni services are offered."

Q: How about for programs in general?
A: "Any student applying to a graduate program in creative writing

should think about what he or she most wants from the program. Ideally, first on the list will be developing the tools to become a better writer, as opposed to, say, getting a book contract. If being trained to teach creative writing, or composition, being trained to work as an editor, or some other related skill is also important to the student, that will help to narrow the list of suitable programs."

Q: Advice for low-residency students?
A: "I'm not sure the advice for low-residency students is all that different from the advice for a residential one: Devote yourself to the work; read broadly and deeply; experiment; and learn as much as possible from your reading, from your fellow students and their writing, and from the faculty, without getting distracted by opportunities for publication and awards, minor contradictions, negative criticism, self-doubt, despair, and other matters of ego. Low-residency students may have to work harder to overcome shyness during the residencies, so as to have face-to-face discussions with students and faculty, and they should also maintain phone or email contact with some of the other students. There's no secret to success, though; hard work is repaid."

Q: Thoughts on your MFA experience?
A: "I earned my MFA at the University of Arizona, where I also had a teaching assistantship. In those days TAs taught two sections of composition every semester; as a result, I felt more like a composition instructor than a writer. That changed toward the end of my time there, as I got to teach creative writing, but the teaching load certainly detracted from the experience. On the other hand, I've had work as a teacher ever since, so I certainly got something from it. . . . Strange as this may sound, and with all respect to the people who tried to teach me, I'm not sure I developed much as a writer while I was at Arizona. I learned a few important lessons, but it took a long time for them to take effect. Perhaps the most influential part of the experience was the interaction with other student writers, many of whom are still colleagues and friends today."

Q: What do teachers want for and from their students?
A: "I'll speak for myself: I hope my students will be inspired, gain a better understanding of what fiction can be and how individual pieces of fiction work, and see and implement new possibilities for

their own work. Ideally, the student will have an impressive combination of talent, intelligence, enthusiasm, curiosity, dedication, conscientiousness, and perseverance. A sense of humor and decency is a bonus."

ᴑᴄᴧᴑ

Padma Viswanathan is a student in the MFA fiction program at the University of Arizona. She holds an MA degree in creative writing from the Johns Hopkins University, and is currently at work on a historical novel set in south India, tentatively titled *Thangam.* **Previous works include the plays** *House of Sacred Cows, Disco Does Not Suck,* **and** *By Air, By Water, By Wood.* **She is also a freelance journalist.**

Q: What are the advantages and disadvantages of attending small or large programs?
A: "I'm still in touch with my classmates from Johns Hopkins. In a smaller program you'll work with the same people during a substantial arc of your, and their, development. My experience is the better you get to know someone, the better responder you can be to their work. I guess the downside of a smaller program is that one very aggressive or even crazy person can spoil it for everyone. I didn't have that experience at all at Hopkins. But I'd expect that one person can really turn the workshop dynamic on its head. . . . For larger programs, on a very basic level, there are more people, and that might increase your chances of finding literary kindred spirits."

Q: Should students change their criteria when it comes to decision time?
A: "I felt like my criteria were the same. Except that the discussions I had with students—I spoke with three from each program—clarified whether the program met those criteria. You definitely get a feel for the teachers, the other students, the resources, and the culture."

Q: Thoughts on the teaching experience as a graduate student?
A: "Teaching composition has taught me how to teach composition. I wanted teaching experience, and that was one reason I went to an MFA program. But teaching literature as a part of a creative writing course makes me a better writer, as does reading good work

by classmates. And being in workshop *is* teacher training. You're practicing how to teach.

Q: Thoughts on workshop and literature classes?
A: I do think the best way to learn how to write is through close reading of excellent writing. This is one reason I, like many people, have some reservations about the workshop process as a way of teaching writers. It's strange to me when people take two workshops per semester and then don't do much of the reading in their literature classes. That seems wrong to me."

∽ↈↈ

Maria Hummel is currently a Wallace Stegner Fellow in poetry at Stanford University. She received her MFA in creative writing from the University of North Carolina at Greensboro. She is the author of the novel *Wilderness Run*.

Q: What is a helpful mind-set for graduate students?
A: "One of the greatest things I learned from my fellow classmates was that this was a time to experiment. It was not a time to narrow down what my idea of a poem was. It was a time to broaden that idea. I had to open myself to as many styles and writers as possible. My advice is to go in with an open mind. This is a time to splash paint all over the walls and see what happens."

Q: What *shouldn't* students expect from a creative writing graduate program?
A: "It's not going to be the golden road to a published book. I remember talking with someone a few years back who said, 'I already know how to write, so I just want to go where the professors are famous. I just need their connections to get my book published.' That's wrongheaded. You shouldn't go unless you've got something to learn."

Q: Thoughts on motivation?
A: "You shouldn't expect that anyone is going to persuade you to love your writing and keep you going at it. It always comes down to your own self-motivation. You can certainly get a lot of support and feedback in a program, but no one outside of yourself is going to make you become a writer."

Q: What did you learn from working as a teaching assistant?
A: "I was a teaching assistant for Fred Chappell in a modern poetry class. I didn't actually have many responsibilities outside of teaching when he was away on book tour and grading papers. Fred is an old master of the lecture, and in class I'd sit and listen to him and take copious notes. I still pull out those notes whenever I have to instruct on someone like Auden or Kipling. It was a useful experience: watching a professor lead a room, but not being a student in the class. Not only did I hear his insights, but I got to observe how to teach."

Q: What about life after a graduate program?
A: "As long as I'm writing every day, as long as I make that appointment with myself, I feel like a writer. It doesn't matter what job I have, as long as I'm writing for some period of time. It's also important to keep up with a community as best you can. Keep up with your classmates, and try to build new networks wherever you next move. . . . It's a little strange: when I published a novel several years after the program, I started to lose my identity as a poet. None of my current friends were poets. They were fiction writers, journalists, screenwriters. Then I made a friend who was a poet, and when we started having conversations about poetry, it was like coming back from another country and remembering my native tongue again. For so long, I'd only been having those conversations with myself."

❧

Geoffrey Wolff is the director of the graduate fiction program at the University of California Irvine. He is the author of four works of nonfiction, including *The Art of Burning Bridges*, *Black Sun*, and *The Duke of Deception*, and six novels, most recently *The Age of Consent*. He is recipient of the Award in Literature from the American Academy of Arts and Letters.

Q: What is a helpful mind-set for creative writing graduate students?
A: "I think principally to keep their eyes on the near term, not the long run. Gazing afar at publication rather than squinting at composition is inevitably blinding. If students will pay close attention to what's in front of them, they'll leave as better writers and certainly

as better readers. Much of writing is a kind of long-haul trucking. Learning how long it takes to get better can be a rude surprise. Stamina and character are as important as natural talent."

Q: Thoughts on letters of recommendation?
A: "Applicants are at the mercy of their recommenders. They need three letters, and it's not uncommon for some endorsers not to write the letters they've agreed to write. Maybe they forget. Maybe they can't think of anything nice to say. Inasmuch as these letters are often sent directly to the schools, the applicant may be left in the dark about an incomplete file. On the other side, we frequently receive such careful and passionately encouraging endorsements that the students who have provoked such enthusiasm would be touched to see them. You want to ask people who know you, yes. And you want to ask people you can count on."

Q: How important is funding to a student's experience?
A: "It can be a problem in many programs. You have two people in workshop: One has a tuition waiver and a $20,000 stipend, another pays full tuition of $35,000. They each bring a story or poem into workshop. It's difficult for students not to look at the work and think 'This story is $55,000 better than this other story?' At UCI [University of California–Irvine] we insist on subtracting financial competition from the cultural equation. Our bedrock principle is that what one person gets is what everyone gets. This has a benign effect on morale."

Q: What if a student is not accepted anywhere? What advice would you offer?
A: "I look at the writing I was doing as an undergraduate. I wouldn't have come within a country mile of being accepted to UCI. I was pretentious, and I was trying to make music. Some people develop very slowly. I think most writers know when they've turned a corner. They know something has happened. For others, they pursue the MFA because their best grades in undergraduate were in creative writing classes. Well, good grades are cheap in undergraduate creative writing classes. That's not enough. Someone who is serious will be addicted to reading, and be able to display the fruits of that passion in his or her application. . . . Finally, the failure of a piece of work or an application is not prophetic. Repeated often enough

it can be, but it's not necessarily so. Writing is an accumulation of failures until—maybe, no guarantee—you begin to get it right."

Q: Thoughts on workshop?
A: "Stability is important in a workshop. The class must have integrity. This begins with the instructor but radiates through the group. Stability enables candor. If good will is assumed, you don't have to be hesitant in giving or receiving judgments. Really, a program's determining factor is the good character and intelligence of its colleagues. Once a program begins to draw good students, they recruit one another."

✖

Quotes in this work also used from the following:

Steve Almond is a graduate of the MFA program at the University of North Carolina Greensboro, and he teaches creative writing at Boston College. His works include *The Evil B.B. Chow, Candyfreak, My Life in Heavy Metal*, and the forthcoming *Which Brings Me to You: A Novel in Confessions.*

Thomas E. Kennedy teaches in the MFA program at Fairleigh Dickinson University, and he is a graduate of the MFA program at Vermont College. His many works include the novels *Kerrigan's Copenhagen, Unreal City*, and *Crossing Borders*, the story collections *Murphy's Angel* and *Drive, Dive, Dance & Fight*, and books about writing, including *Realism & Other Illusions: Essays on the Craft of Fiction.*

APPENDIX B

Reading Lists

At one point I'd created a list of novels, nonfiction books, poetry books, craft books, and the like to include here, but I found this too prescriptive. Who to leave on? Who to leave off? What sorts of styles are being promoted here? I felt that such a list would become a bit of a lightning rod of criticism for *this* book (writers and friends of writers can be a touchy sort), and the integrity of this book and its contents are important to me. That said, I've included here links to reading lists compiled by various individuals, organizations, and programs.

The reading lists of the Gotham Writers Workshop, in particular, are as impressive, comprehensive, and updated as any lists I've found on the Web. There are terrific subcategories in each genre that include the actual creative works, books about craft, anthologies, periodicals, reference, and era. Definitely worth a visit by any prospective student or reader.

A reading list in just about every genre. Updated and comprehensive. From the **Gotham Writers Workshop**— http://www.writingclasses.com/WritersResources/resources.php.

The **Arizona State University English Department** list in poetry, fiction and playwriting. Links are on the bottom right, in tiny font— http://www.asu.edu/creativewriting/rdglists/.

The **UNC Wilmington MFA Program** reading list in fiction, poetry, creative nonfiction, and playwriting. This is a PDF file.—http://www.uncwil.edu/writers/documents/MFAreadinglist.pdf.

Sue William Silverman offers one of the best nonfiction reading lists anywhere. From the University of Iowa Nonfiction page—http://www.english.uiowa.edu/nonfiction/readinglist.html.

The **University of Alaska Fairbanks** reading lists in poetry, fiction, and nonfiction—http://www.uaf.edu/english/degreesoffered/compind.html.

Bruce Dobler, of the University of Pittsburgh offers a list for creative nonfiction—http://www.pitt.edu/~bdobler/brieflist.html.

The **San Jose State University MFA Program** reading list in fiction, poetry, creative nonfiction, and playwriting— http://www2.sjsu.edu/depts/english/MFA/reading_list.html.

Lighthouse has a terrific site for screenwriters, with links to many other sites—http://www.lighthouse.org.uk/pages/film_and_video/networks_and_links/projects/Screenwriting.php.

The **University of St. Louis** undergraduate reading lists in fiction and poetry—http://www.umsl.edu/divisions/artscience/english/creative/readinglist.html.

The **Brooklyn College MFA program** reading list in fiction, playwriting, and poetry—http://depthome.brooklyn.cuny.edu/english/graduate/mfa/r_ist.htm.

The **Western Illinois University Theatre Department** offers a list for the MFA in theatre—http://www.wiu.edu/theatre/mfaexam-readinglist.shtml.

William Ronald Craig of MovieMind has a list of how-to books on screenwriting—http://www.screenwritinghelp.com/bMoMind-ReadList.html

APPENDIX C

Helpful Sources Online

As of summer 2008 these sites were up and running . . .

I decided to take the "Complete List of Programs" out of this second edition. By the time the book is a year old, the list has changed. So, here are two excellent sources for you to access online. **Associated Writing Programs** is an organization that supports writers and writing organizations around the world. They publish (for free, now on the Web!) the very helpful *AWP Official Guide to Writing Programs*—http://guide.awpwriter.org/.

Anna Mendoza has the most up-to-date listings of MFA programs, both traditional and low-residency. Visit her blogs at http://creative-writingmfa.blogspot.com/ and http://lowresmfa.blogspot.com/.

The "Complete List of Programs" from first edition of this *Handbook* is available at *http://creative-writing-mfa-handbook.blog-spot.com/2008/05/mfa-programs-listing-from-first-edition.html.*

A must visit is to the Poets & Writers Toolbox. Lots of information here about MFA programs, literary magazines, and writers conferences at http://www.pw.org/toolsforwriters.

Also, make sure you log into the *Speakeasy Forum* at Poets & Writers. Here you'll meet many writers, students, and teachers. This is one of the best online sources available for information about programs and writing, at http://www.pw.org/connect.

Our own MFA blog is available by typing "MFA Blog" into Google, or at http://creative-writing-mfa-handbook.blogspot.com/.

Seth Abramson, who wrote chapter 3 of this book, has a terrific site called The Suburban Ecstasies. You can access all sorts of new data and statistics about MFA programs at http://sethabramson. blogspot.com/.

Erika Dreifus has a wonderful site called The Practicing Writer. For more great insights and information from Erika, please visit http://www.practicing-writer.com/.

All sorts of MFA rankings are available at http://mfarankings.blog-spot.com/.

One of my favorite sites on the Web is Wake Up Writing. It has a new writing exercise each morning at http://www.wakeupwriting. com/.

After the MFA is a terrific site for post-, pre-, and current graduate students at http://www.afterthemfa.com/.

Articles from Rick Moody and Edward J. Delaney reflect on the MFA world at http://www.theatlantic.com/doc/200508/moody and http://www.theatlantic.com/doc/200708/edward-delaney-mfa.

Some interviews with me about the book, blog, and programs can be found at http://www.thepublishingspot.com/2006/04/five_easy_ questions_tom_kealey.html and http://www.52projects.com/52_ projects/2006/04/the_inspiration.html.

OTHER LISTINGS AND RANKINGS

The listing of the *U.S. News and World Report* **1997 Rankings** (thanks to Albert Rouzie)—http://www-as.phy.ohiou.edu/~rouzie/569A/compcreative/University.htm.

Web del Sol has a Creative Writing Project linking surfers to specific programs and universities—http://webdelsol.com/CWP/.

The **Modern Language Association** promotes the study and teaching of language and literature at universities—http://www.mla.org/homepage.

Drowning Man has a comprehensive list of literary publications—http://www.drowningman.net/.

The **Nebraska Center for Writers** includes information on programs in-state and across the country, as well as a helpful links section—http://mockingbird.creighton.edu/NCW/cwp.htm.

ADVICE

Angela Jane Fountas answers a few MFA questions on the Seattle Writer Grrls site—http://www.seattlewritergrrls.org/archive/2001i3_mfahelp.htm.

And Jane's main website, **Write Habit**, is an excellent resource for a variety of writing questions and answers—http://www.writehabit.org/.

Suzanne Keen has written a terrific article about English Literature graduate programs—http://english.wlu.edu/program/gradschool.htm.

. . . as has **Linda Troost**—http://www.washjeff.edu/users/ltroost/GradSchool.html.

The **University of Oregon** has the best FAQ page I've seen from programs. Though many questions are U of O specific, many are not—http://darkwing.uoregon.edu/~crwrweb/faq.htm.

American Book Publishing has a helpful article titled "Is an MFA Program Right for You?"—http://www.american-book.com/Articles/aredvargus2.htm.

Joseph Schuster looks at the academic marketplace regarding creative writing programs—http://www.webster.edu/~schustjm/creative.htm.

Kevin Clark offers advice for potential MFA students—http://cla.calpoly.edu/~kclark-mfaqa.html.

The **Writers House and Career Services at UPenn** sent out a questionnaire about writing programs to graduate students and faculty. Nine people responded, and their insightful comments are here—http://www.vpul.upenn.edu/careerservices/gradprof/grad/gradmfa_writing.htm.

BLOGS ABOUT WRITING

Moby Lives—http://mobylives.com/.

Maud Newton—http://maudnewton.com/blog/.

Bookslut—http://www.bookslut.com/.

The Elegant Variation—http://marksarvas.blogs.com/elegvar/.

Beatrice—http://beatrice.com/.

The Moorish Girl is an excellent literary blog in its own right, and it also has a link page to other literary blogs—http://www.moorishgirl.com/.

OTHER

For listings of poetry book contests, visit the **Poetry Society of America**—http://www.poetrysociety.org/psa-links.php.

Poetry Daily. One new poem every day. A great site—http://www.poems.com/.

Poewar.com has an eclectic mix of writing-related links—http://poewar.com/articles/.

FASA. The Application for Federal Student Aid—http://www.fafsa.ed.gov/.

Jacob Javits Fellowship. A national fellowship for graduate students—http://www.ed.gov/programs/jacobjavits/index.html.

The **University of Minnesota** lists postgraduate fellowships and opportunities—http://english.cla.umn.edu/creativewriting/announcements/jobs.html.

Shaw Guides provides listings of writers conferences and workshops—http://writing.shawguides.com/.

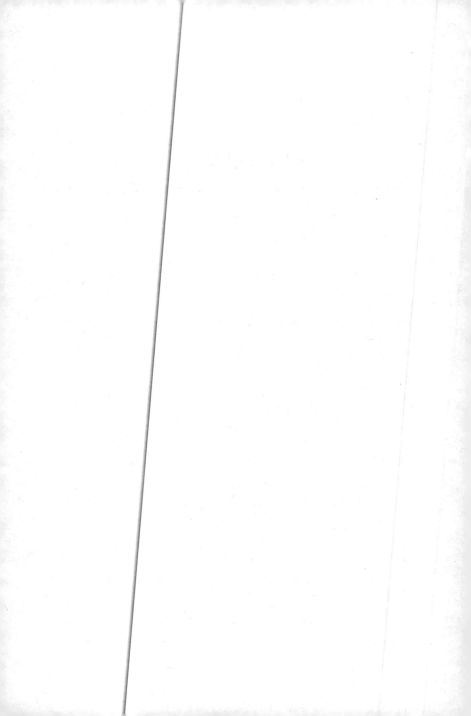

MFA Blog Tip Sheet

From http://creative-writing-mfa-handbook.blogspot.com

1. If you can afford it, apply to between eight and twelve programs. The selection process is unpredictable. Keep your options open.

2. Quit whining about not wanting to take the GRE. Take the GRE: it will expand your potential program list. Your GRE scores won't factor much into the selection, but you can't apply at a lot of programs without them.

3. You'll need some combination of writing samples, a personal statement, letters of recommendation, GRE scores, undergraduate transcripts, and maybe a couple other items. Your writing sample will count for about 90% of your acceptance or rejection, so be sure to make it count.

4. Don't ask the blog about whether you should apply in fiction, poetry, screenwriting, or any other genre. How are we supposed to know? Apply in the genre you're most excited about.

5. Ask for letters of recommendation from people you can count on. (i.e., people who will actually write the letters and who will say nice things about you). Getting someone dependable is more important than getting someone famous. Generally speaking, you'd like to have two letters from teachers and one from a former boss, or editor, or fellow writer. But go with what you've got.

6. When considering programs (and this is my advice, and not often the same advice of many other people), consider location, funding, and teaching experience, in that order. Make a list of places where you'd like to live and where you could stand to live. Think about your financial situation (and don't drop 35K a year on a writing program), and select programs that meet your funding needs. Consider whether you'd like teaching experience or not. Using these three items, you can get your list down from over one hundred to about twenty. Then, factor in program reputation and professors and anything else you deem important.

7. The MFA degree is an artistic degree and not primarily a professional degree. Don't expect that the degree will get you a teaching job and a book deal. Expect that you'll spend two to three years focusing closely on your craft within a writing community. It's an MFA degree, similar to MFA studio art degrees.

8. For your personal statement: Come across as formal and friendly. Come across as a serious writer and a dependable person. Discuss your life experience, your goals, and the reason you want to take this time. The letter should be no more than one and a half to two pages.

9. Once you're accepted (hopefully, at more than one program), get in touch with current students and ask them about the atmosphere there. You'll learn a lot by getting the ground's-eye view.

10. Some programs that I like (regarding reputation and funding) that you might consider (these are in no particular order): Purdue, Massachusetts, Oregon, Iowa, UC-Irvine, Indiana, Syracuse, Johns Hopkins, Michigan, Minnesota, UNCG, UNCW, Virginia, Florida State, Alabama, Arkansas, Florida, Mississippi, Wisconsin, Arizona, Arizona State, and Texas. Low-residency programs include Warren Wilson, Lesley, Antioch, Bennington, and Vermont.

11. Keep in mind that some programs offer five slots a year, while others will offer thirty or more. Try to choose a good mix between small and large programs so that you'll have options.

Acknowledgments

THE PROBLEM WITH ACKNOWLEDGMENT SECTIONS is that you look forward to writing them, but then you normally wait until the day before the book deadline to get them done. That, again, is the case in this edition. Many people to thank. My sincerest apology for anyone I've left out.

David Roderick is a constant source of advice and encouragement, and he makes himself available whenever I have a strange idea or worry. Thanks for everything, brother. Steve Elliott is always around to lift spirits, offer new perspectives, and in general be a good example of what a writer is and does. Chellis Ying and Laurie Sandell help keep my head on straight. Jack and Helen Kealey and their daughter Kerri seemed, to me at least, blindly optimistic when they said "You'll get it done," though they were, to my great shock and surprise, correct. Thanks to them, and other members of the Kealey and Carroll families who have been so supportive over the years.

Katharine Noel, as I recall, was the first person to say, "That's a great idea," before I actually thought that it was. She was also a great sounding board and source of encouragement, especially in the dangerous early days of the project. In the late dangerous days of the project, that person was Christina McCarroll, who was consistently generous with her time and suggestions. Katie Boyle is a wonderful agent and person, and believed in this book from the get-go. Many thanks to her, and David Barker and all the people at Continuum Publishing.

The individuals interviewed for the book were extremely generous with their time, insights, and ideas. Their knowledge and contributions often went far beyond the scope of my questions. I asked many for fifteen minutes and received hours of their time instead. Very special thanks to Aimee Bender, Michael Collier, Victoria Chang, Johanna Foster, Maria Hummel, Rachel Kadish, Scott McCabe, Heather McHugh, George Saunders, Tracy K. Smith, Bruce Snider, Peter Turchi, Padma Viswanathan, and Geoffrey Wolff. Rachel, Bruce, and especially Johanna were of great help to me not only during the interviews but throughout the course of this project.

I would be remiss if I did not thank my former writing teachers. If there is any knowledge in this book, or in the writing of it, much of it comes from them. Very special thanks to Fred Chappell, John Edgar Wideman, Tobias Wolff, Sam Michel, Noy Holland, Elizabeth Tallent, David MacDonald, Jay Neugeboren, and especially to John L'Heureux.

Thanks also to many of my colleagues, whom I've pestered for opinions, insights, research, and support over the years. Early on in my career I counted heavily on Nick Montemarano, Susan Steinberg, and especially Cathy Schlund-Vials. Others who have helped this book in large and small ways are Andrew Altschul, Shara Lessley, Robin Ekiss, Keith Ekiss, Cheryl McGrath, Tom McNeely, Lysley Tenorio, Gaby Calvocoressi, Geoff Brock, Scott Hutchins, Rachel Richardson, Eric Puchner, Sara Martin, Russ Franklin, John Lundberg, Marika Ismail, Malena Watrous, and Geri Doran. Very special thanks to Adam and Stephanie. Lately I've also received much help from Chellis Ying, Josh Tyree, Skip Horack, Molly Antopol-Johnson, Chanan Tigay, Bruce Snider, Emily Mitchell, Gravity Goldberg, Isaac Fitzgerald, Laurie Sandell, Maria Hummel, Shimon Tanaka, and Rachel Kadish.

Thanks also to many supportive people at Stanford not yet mentioned, including Mary Popek, Ryan Jacobs, Gay Pierce, Virginia Hess, Matt Jockers, Ruth Kaplan, Jeremy Sabol, Megan Miller, and especially Eavan Boland.

General spirit-lifters include Eric and Ashly Morrison, Shaila Djurovich, Kristy Byrd, Matt Alper, Sarah Hinds, Ben Peterson, Wendy McKennon, Christine Texiera, Dawn McAvoy, Chris Kirkman, Allison Jones, Sandy Chang, Dorothy Hans, Michael Breen, Meena Wilson, Tommy and Kelcie Beaver, and Steadman and Alyssa Harrison. Also very special thanks to Phil Knight and Mark Purcell.